NEGOTIATE

NEGOTIATE

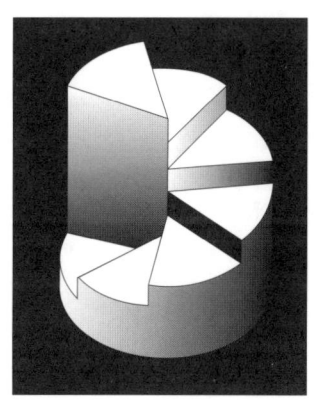

The Seven Step Master Plan.

Harry Mills

THE MILLS GROUP

First publication 1991. Reprinted 1992, 1994, 1997
THE MILLS GROUP
P O Box 30-818 Lower Hutt
New Zealand

Limpbound ISBN 0-908722-80-X

Other Editions:
Gower Publishing Group, England
Executive World Book Club, England
Reed Academic Publishing Asia, Singapore
Makron Books, Brazil
Teknisk Forlag, Denmark
Binarupa Aksara, Indonesia

Edited by Michael Keith
Typeset by Wordset Enterprises Ltd, Wellington
Printed in Hong Kong through Bookprint Consultants, Wellington

Contents

Acknowledgements

So many people have contributed to my learning on negotiation over the years I now find it a great struggle to say exactly where a particular idea originated. I do, however, want to thank David Lax, Roger Fisher and the staff at the Harvard Negotiation Project who were so generous with their ideas and time during my visit with them in 1988.

I owe a tremendous debt to my many clients and seminar participants who have helped to test and refine the materials.

I want to especially thank all those who agreed to review the manuscript in its various drafts. I will thank people here in alphabetical order: Bruce Anderson, Rosamund Averton, Paul Baines, Mike Bayliss, Paul Bebbington, Jacob Bercovitch, Wendy Betteridge, Richard Braczek, Tom Broadmore, William Brown, Dave Butler, Rob Cameron, Murray Campbell, Kate Clark, Chris Collett, Linda Craig, Alastair Davis, Lee Davis, Colin Douglas, Jim Doyle, Dave Elliott, Glen Evans, Martyn Fisher, David Ford, Mark Ford, Rod Gillespie, Roy Glass, Mike Heenan, Bob Henare, Garrie Hoddinott, Gordon Holmes, Shelley Hood, John Howell, Alan Jones, Irene Joyce, Ian Kennedy, Roger Kerr, Kristine Kilkelly, Sally Kincaid, Andy Kirkland, Alan Koziarski, Sheryl Kruger, Dick Lang, Tony Lawson, Gary

Lloydd, Jim McClean, Mark McDonald, Alasdair MacLeod, Doug Martin, Mike Menzies, Gerald Minee, Howard Moore, Craig Morris, Graham Nahkies, Richard Norman, Doug Pender, Karen Poutasi, Lyn Provost, Fiona Pyke, Claire Reiher, Johnathon Ross, Phil Ryan, Barry Saunders, Julia Scott, Richard Somerville-Ryan, Paul Steere, Carol Stigley, Andrew Strange, Mike Suggate, Doug Taylor, Peter Taylor, Bob Thompson, Alison Timms, Dame Cath Tizard, Susan Toder, Brian Trigger, Denis Urlich, Patti Vessell, Bob Vine, Jane Warren, David Wilkins, Bryce Wilkinson, Lee Wilkinson, Derek Williams, Sherwyn Williams, James Willis, Bill Wilson, John Young.

I had the finest secretarial help imaginable. Thanks to Janice Tomlin for her total commitment, moral support and endless patience. Two other staff, Alyson Howell and Wanda Peck, also deserve special thanks for their support and cheerfulness.

Finally, there is my wife, Mary Anne. Her love and support has never waivered. Without these the book would never have been possible. She has now put up with me for 11 books and that alone demands special acknowledgement.

Introduction

Before I started writing this book I drew up a list of the features I believed a negotiation handbook should contain.

First and foremost a negotiation handbook has to be *practical*. A handbook must not only be interesting, it must be useful. The tips, techniques and strategies should have been field tested and the examples drawn from real life.

A handbook must be *user-friendly*. Information must be readable and easily accessed. The test of a good handbook is how fast you can access the information you're searching for. A user friendly handbook has a comprehensive list of contents, a good index, lots of subheadings, checklists of key points, and is attractively designed.

However while effective handbooks are simple to follow, they are never simplistic. Negotiation is a complex subject which takes time to master. Authors who reduce the subject to four or five key commandments or principles do their readers a disservice.

A negotiation handbook whose goal is to help readers become better negotiators must focus on the *skills* it takes to become a top negotiator. Anyone who has run skill based negotiation seminars knows it is not enough to tell participants to ask questions and actively listen. You also have to show them *how* to question and listen. An effective negotiation handbook must do the same.

The central thrust in any negotiation handbook should be on how to facilitate win-win negotiations. This is not simply a matter of ethical preference, it is good business. The vast majority of negotiations most people find themselves in are situations where it is in their self interest to create a solution which is good for both sides. Negotiations, based on *mutual* satisfaction, work better, are essential for long-term relationships and lead to repeat business.

Nevertheless, life in the real world means you also have to negotiate with ruthless or unethical operators. A hand-book which ignores this fact and doesn't show you how to cope or urges you to rely on trust and goodwill is naive and dangerous.

Since no single publication on negotiation contained all the features I looked for, I decided to write *Negotiate: The Seven Step Master Plan*.

The book is organised around the seven identifiable steps which make up the negotiation process. Apart from the logic of starting at the beginning with the preparation step and ending up with how to tie-up the loose ends, the steps are a useful memory and training aid. Different skills and abilities are used in each step. And once you can identify what step you are in you can plan your course of action. In-experienced negotiators often skip out the early steps, rush into trading concessions, lose control and end up with a bad deal.

Negotiators who follow the seven steps and who can iden-tify what they need to do, keep control. Control breeds con-fidence and results in even better deals.

CHAPTER ONE

Walking The Negotiator's Tightrope

"When a man tells me he's
going to put all his cards on the table,
I always look up his sleeve."

Lord (Issac) Leslie-Hore-Belisha

We have been negotiating for thousands of years since the time our stone age ancestors traded stone flints for skins.

Given this background and the fact that every one of us negotiates virtually every day of our lives, you might expect that by now we would be skilled negotiators. Regrettably, this is not so. Wars continue breaking out, strikes still plague industrial relations, divorce rates stand at a record high, while the courts are clogged up with business litigation.

Why then do we find it so hard to negotiate well? The answer lies in the very nature of negotiation.

First, negotiators must walk a tightrope between total cooperation and naked competition. Negotiators have to weigh up the pros and cons of adopting a tough, demanding, competitive position. You might get the best possible deal for yourself. However you might also turn the other side into an adversary whom you drive away from the negotiation table altogether.

Second, negotiators must walk a tightrope between openness and honesty, secrecy and misrepresentation. There are very few negotiating situations where you can afford to be completely open and honest without risking being exploited by the other side. In a negotiation you can never be sure what the other player's cards really are – only what the other party *says* they are. If you disclose the true identity of your cards, then your counterpart can fleece you as cleanly as any skilled pick pocket. On the other hand, if you hold your cards too close to your chest for too long, you risk creating so much mistrust the other party might not negotiate at all.[1]

Third, negotiators must walk a tightrope between short term advantages and long term gains. If you play tough and aggressive, it is often possible to score a quick victory – at the other side's expense. However, when the other side reflects on their defeat, the relationship quickly sours – and the possibility of long term gains disappears. It often pays to accept a little less than you could have won – simply because of the trust it encourages and other potential long term gains.

Adopt the wrong approach in negotiations and the consequences can be disastrous. International real estate consultant Doug Malouf learnt his first lesson in negotiation basics the hard way – as he relates in this tale about Mrs Fittler and the eggs.

Every January, Mum and Dad would pack up and head for their favourite hotel in town. They would stay there while Dad did his buying for the next year from a wholesaler named Hoffnung.

The year I turned 17 they set off for town as usual, leaving a manager in charge of the store. They left me there, too, waiting for my chance to make my first executive decision. A 17-year-old time bomb waiting to explode.

One day I was left in charge for a few hours. It was a Tuesday. And every Tuesday for 20 years Mrs Fittler had come into the store to sell my father a dozen eggs. Now, you must understand that supply and demand had nothing to do with this transaction. It was just something Mrs Fittler did. Every Tuesday she came into town and sold my dad, Nicholas Malouf, a dozen eggs.

So there I was, in charge. And in came Mrs Fittler with her eggs. The eggs were fresh but my relationship with Mrs Fittler was rotten. We'd just never got on.

She walked up to the counter and held out her package. "Good morning," she said. "Here are your eggs."

Poor Mrs Fittler. She hadn't realised yet that it was Doug Malouf, the hard-nosed businessman and master negotiator, that she was dealing with this time. We already had plenty of eggs. I was in a position of strength. So I let her have it between the eyes. "We don't want your eggs."

She didn't seem to notice the crushing blow I'd dealt her.

She just fixed me with one unblinking eye. "Where's your father?" she said. "He's been buying my eggs for 20 years."

This was the moment of truth. I had the power to make decisions and I was going to use it.

"My father is in town . . . and I'm the boss. And we don't need your eggs."

She looked at me again without any signs of emotion. She still didn't realise that I'd won. "Is that your final word?"

"Yes," I said. My cousin Betty in accounts had been watching what was happening. Why was she smiling?

Mrs Fittler walked across to her. "Betty, I'd like you to make up my account . . . and the Cassiday's, and the Jarriday's, and all the other Fittler accounts. It'll save them a trip."

Have you got any idea of what it's like to be 17 and to have just cost your father's business its best five accounts . . . plus another six that weren't all that bad either? Believe me, a wisdom tooth extraction without anaesthetic looks attractive by comparison.

Suicide becomes a genuine option. Mrs Fittler clearly didn't understand the laws of supply and demand. She didn't notice that I was in a position of negotiating strength. She just closed 11 accounts and left the store.

Betty was very supportive. "Just wait till your father gets back," she said. "He'll kill you."

Actually, he didn't kill me. He was very understanding. He discussed the matter calmly and outlined the options available to me. "Get the accounts back," he said, "or don't bother to come home."

When I got off my bike and walked up to Mrs Fittler's front door, there she was framed in the doorway. The theme from "High Noon" filled the room behind her.

Things didn't look good. I didn't have to open my mouth.

"Your father sent you, didn't he?" she barked.

I nodded.

"Let me tell you something, son. I'm coming back to your father's store. But it's only because he's such a good man. I wouldn't want to hurt him because he's got a fool for a son."

What could I say?

"There are the eggs," she said. She was right. The eggs were there. The same eggs she'd brought in three weeks ago. Wrapped in the same newspaper. You didn't need to be able to see them to know they were there. I took a long look at them.

"Well, make up your mind," she said. "Do you want them or not?" She had me, and she knew it. The master negotiator had been beaten.

I picked them up delicately and turned to go. She stopped me and handed me another parcel. "Here's two dozen more for the last two weeks. Make sure your father gets them . . . all of them."

Always consider the feelings of the people you are doing business with. If you offend or humiliate them they're not likely to deal with you now . . . or in the future.

When you are doing business, there doesn't have to be a loser. In fact, everyone should win if the business is conducted properly. The best possible outcome is a sale that leaves everyone satisfied.[2]

This book shows you how to walk the negotiator's tightrope and at the same time put together win-win agreements which last.

In the meantime, keep your eyes open for Mrs Fittler. And make sure you buy her eggs.

CHAPTER TWO

Everyone Negotiates

*"When a person with money
meets a person with experience, the person
with the experience winds up with the money
and the person with money ends up
with the experience."*

Harvey Mackay

What is Negotiation?

We all negotiate because negotiation is simply a very effective way of getting what we want. We negotiate to settle our differences and we negotiate out of self-interest to satisfy our needs.

In a negotiation both sides have common interests and conflicting interests. Unless both are present, a negotiation is pointless. Although numerous differences or conflicting interests separate the USSR and the USA, both negotiate rather than fight because of the common interests they share in reducing the costs and dangers of an uncontrolled arms race.

We only negotiate when the alternative to negotiation, that is, no agreement, is worse. Unions strike rather than negotiate because they believe a strike will result in greater gains than talks. Employers lock out their workers, nations fight each other and litigants battle each other in court for similar reasons.

We often confuse negotiation with other forms of conflict resolution. You know you are in negotiation if you have the authority and ability to vary the terms – to give as well as take. Negotiations, in essence, involve trading concessions.

Negotiation is, therefore, much more than persuasion. You can try to persuade a difficult employee to mend his ways, but unless you can vary the terms and commit resources you are merely discussing or arguing your way through a problem.

Talking for Money

Every day we negotiate. Yet few of us appreciate what we could begin to achieve if we could negotiate to our full potential.

In my negotiation seminars I begin by extolling the virtues of turning conflict into agreement. Everyone, it seems, wants to be able to close more sales, build long-term working relationships and be better able to identify customer and clients needs.

With business audiences, interest always picks up when I demonstrate the impact of negotiating skills on profits. Look at the sales and costs figures shown opposite for Xirex Industries.

1. The sales staff, by negotiating an across the board price increase of 1%, increased income by \$2,018,000 (1% of \$201,800,000).

2. The buyers, by negotiating a price cut in supplies by 1%, saved \$622,000 (1% of \$62,200,000).

3. Personnel, by negotiating labour savings of 1%, saved $800,000 (1% of $80,000,000).
4. Add these savings up and profits increase by 21%. And that 21% rise in profits is achieved without producing one extra ounce of product.

No wonder negotiators claim it is easier to talk for money than work for it.

Xirex Industries

	Initial Figures	After a 1% Improvement in Sales/Costs
1. Total Sales	201,800,000	203,818,000
2. Total Purchases	62,200,000	61,578,000
3. Employee Costs	80,000,000	79,200,000
Total Other Costs	43,200,000	43,200,000
Total Costs	185,400,000	183,978,000
4. Profits Before Tax	16,400,000	19,840,000

I have yet to find any person, company or non-profit organisation who can't improve their negotiation results at least one percent. Five to ten percent is much more common.

If a manager on an annual salary of $55,000 negotiates a five percent increase in wages and conditions, he pockets an extra $110,000 over a working life of 40 years. Do the same calculation on yourself.

R-E-S-P-E-C-T
The seven steps to agreement

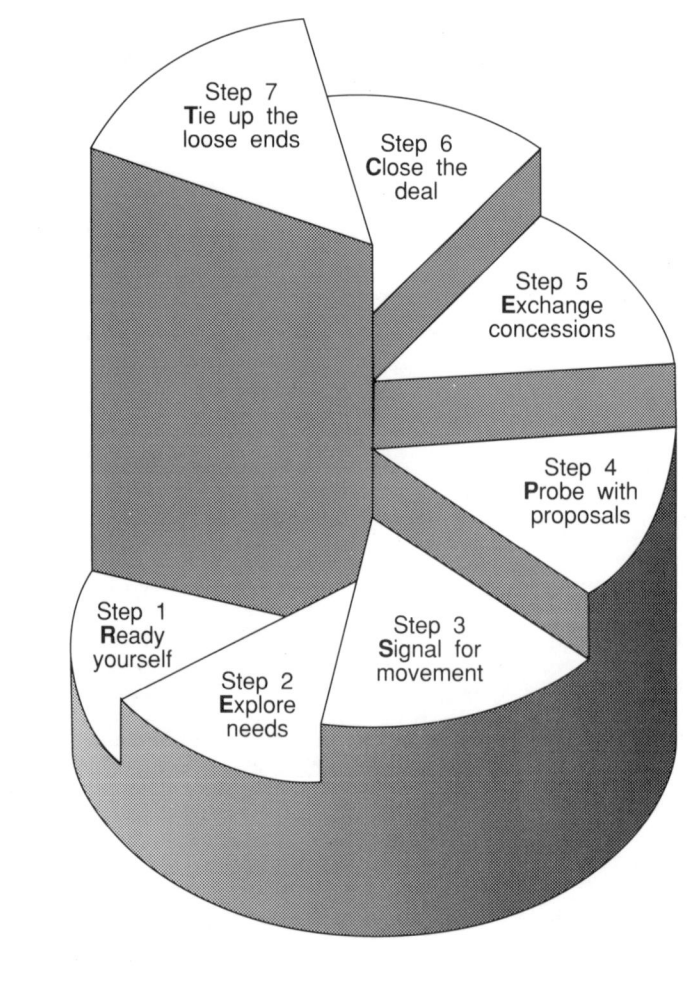

Step 7
Tie up the
loose ends

Step 6
Close the
deal

Step 5
Exchange
concessions

Step 4
Probe with
proposals

Step 1
Ready
yourself

Step 2
Explore
needs

Step 3
Signal for
movement

CHAPTER THREE

R-E-S-P-E-C-T: The Seven Steps to Agreement

"An objective without a plan is a dream."

Douglas McGregor

The negotiation process can be broken into seven identifiable steps which form the acronym RESPECT.

In the process of reaching agreement, negotiators move back and forth between the steps spending varying amounts of time in each area. Different skills and abilities are used in each step. Once you can identify what step you are in you can set your course of action.

In Step One you: **Ready** yourself. In the preparation step you:

- Set and prioritise your objectives.
- List the issues.
- Determine what concessions you can give and what concessions you need in return.
- Gather as much information as you can.
- Plan your strategy and supporting tactics.

In Step Two you: **Explore** each other's needs. In the exploration step you meet face-to-face with the other side to:

- Clarify your and the other side's needs.
- Test your assumptions.
- Build rapport to create a win-win climate.
- Communicate your opening position.
- Learn the other side's opening position.

In Step Three you: **Signal** for movement. Because negotiations often begin with both sides taking strong initial positions, to create momentum you have to be able to:

- Signal that you are prepared to move.
- Respond to signals from the other side and build momentum.

In Step Four you: **Probe** with proposals. To advance the negotiation further along you:

- Make tentative proposals in order to probe for points where the other side will make concessions.
- Repackage rejected proposals into a more acceptable form.

In Step Five you: **Exchange** concessions. Here you:

- Trade concessions by giving the other party some, or part, of their demands in exchange for receiving some, or part, of what you want.

In Step Six you: **Close** the deal. To avoid giving away too many concessions you end the bargaining process by:

- Making a credible and acceptable close.

In Step Seven you: **Tie-up** the loose ends. Having agreed you have a deal you must:

- Confirm exactly what has been agreed.
- Summarise the details of the agreement on paper.
- Agree on a plan to settle possible future differences.

A good agreement is one which works and lasts. In essence it is one that leaves both parties satisfied.

The Bargaining Range

As both sides move through the negotiation process and move closer towards each other and agreement, they move into the *The Bargaining Range* or *Zone of Agreement*.

This is best shown in a diagram. Consider an industrialist and property owner negotiating over the price of a warehouse. The owner of the building has asked for $700,000 and will not drop below $400,000 (his reserve price). He does not know it but the industrialist could go up to $500,000 (her reserve price).

The bargaining range runs from the seller's reserve price to the buyer's reserve price. The settlement will be reached somewhere in this Zone of Agreement.

Zone of Agreement

Let's imagine the industrialist's reserve price is only $350,000, while the owner's reserve price is still $400,000. As the diagram overleaf shows, there is now no Zone of Agreement.

No Zone of Agreement

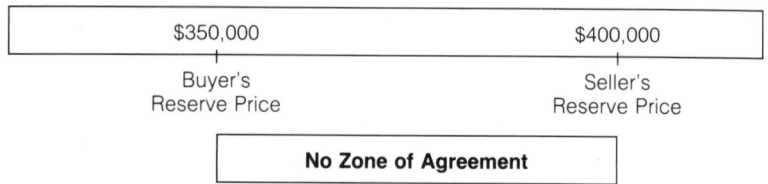

Unless the parties are prepared to move, the negotiation will *deadlock*. Once they are in the bargaining range the two sides can then use their bargaining skills to reach agreement.

R-E-S-P-E-C-T

The seven steps to agreement

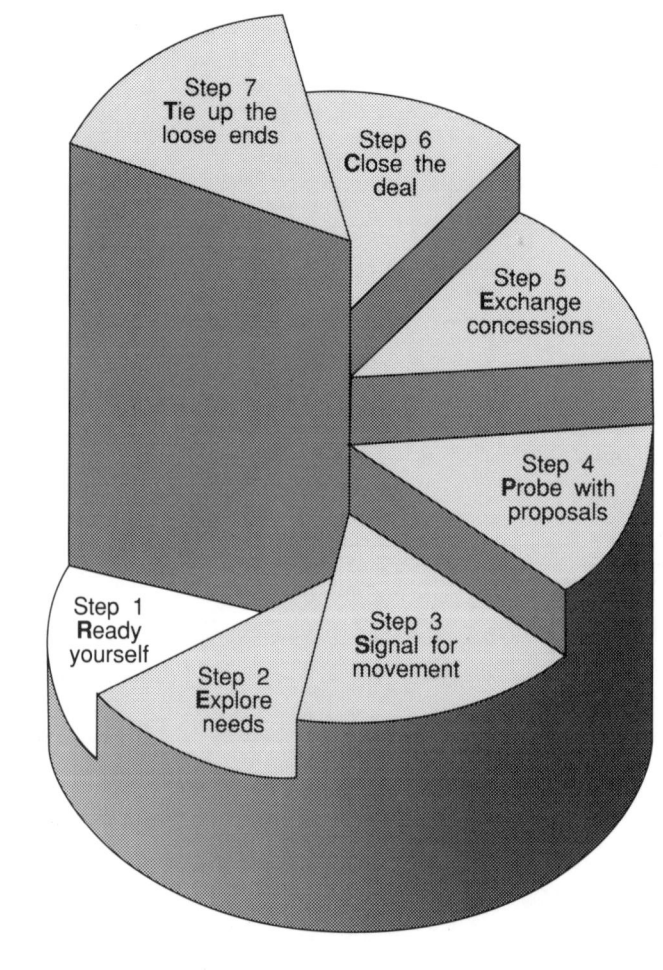

Step 7
Tie up the
loose ends

Step 6
Close the
deal

Step 5
Exchange
concessions

Step 4
Probe with
proposals

Step 1
Ready
yourself

Step 2
Explore
needs

Step 3
Signal for
movement

CHAPTER FOUR

Step One: Readying Yourself

"If I had nine hours to cut down a tree, I would spend six hours sharpening my axe!"

Abraham Lincoln

Attention to detail in the preparation stage of negotiations more often than not marks the difference between success and failure. More negotiations are lost through poor preparation than any other cause. Top negotiators, therefore, always do their homework. They know their business, they know their opponents, they know what they want, and they know how to get it.

In 1972 drought had ravaged the Ukraine grain crop leaving the Russians desperately short of wheat.

The obvious source was the USA, then drowning in a sea of surplus grain. The American government was even paying American farmers not to grow it. And it was trying to discourage other countries from producing more wheat by paying its grain merchants export subsidies whenever the domestic price passed $60 a ton.

On June 29, 1972, a highly trained Russian purchasing team arrived in the United States to embark on the biggest grain buying expedition in history with instructions to buy 20 million plus tons of grain.

The Russians, without indicating the actual size of their intended purchases, asked the US government to keep the news quiet on the pretext they did not want to upset the already volatile commodity markets. The Russians knew that if news of the scale of their purchases leaked out prices would rocket upwards.

Then the Russians summoned Michael Fribourg, owner of Continental Grain, one of America's largest grain companies. The Russians calmly asked Fribourg for his best price on four million tons of wheat. Fribourg could hardly believe his ears. If successful this would be the single biggest grain order ever transacted.

Before giving a price, Fribourg said he would have to check with the US Department of Agriculture to see if export subsidies would continue on sales of this scale – especially as they were to the Russians. The Assistant Secretary of Agriculture for International Affairs, Carroll Brunthaver, assured Fribourg the subsidy would continue. (Brunthaver, who later claimed that he did not check with anyone else in the USDA, had been in the position for just 11 days.)

Fribourg now offered the Russians the wheat for 60 dollars a ton and then quietly began buying up surplus wheat from the many desperate farmers he knew were around.

Meanwhile the Russians played the same game with the other major grain merchants. When the buying bonanza finished in August 1972, the Russians had bought 20 million tons of grain, much of it below the prevailing market rate, for $1.2 billion. It was the grain bargain of the century. When the five US grain giants later filed for their subsidies, the bill for the American taxpayer totalled $316 million.

By the time US Budget Director Casper Weinberger stepped in to order the end of the wheat export subsidy, it was too late. The Russians had purchased all they needed.

In the investigation of the wheat sale which followed, Secretary of Agriculture Butz admitted he had no idea how desperate the Russians were for grain. He had few clues to the size of the sales that were taking place.

The fallout from the deal continued for most of the next year. Because of the shortages wheat prices trebled and shortages in feed grain led to price increases of over 50% for meat and poultry.

President Nixon summed up the effects of being caught unprepared. "We were schnookered," said the President.[3]

The US Department of Agriculture, with the help of US intelligence, should have been monitoring the state of Russian agriculture more closely. Food shortages in Russia were bound to impact on world prices and the scale of subsidies needed to prop up US farmers. Fribourg's call to Carroll Brunthaver should have also sounded warning bells with the USDA that the scale of Russian purchases needed checking out urgently. Even so, you have to admire the thoroughness of the Russians' preparation.

Working Out Your BATNA

Bottom Lines

Most of us have negotiated an agreement which in retrospect we should have rejected. You walk into an antique dealer's shop where a Georgian chair takes your fancy. After a lot of haggling you pay over $1250 after knocking $150 off the list price. When you get home you realise you got carried away. You couldn't really afford $1250. The most you could really afford was $850.

Negotiators commonly protect themselves against pressures and temptations such as these by fixing a bottom line in advance. If you are buying, a bottom line is the highest price you are prepared to pay. If you are selling, a bottom line is the lowest price you will take.

You and your business partner decide, for example, to place your business on the market for $2,000,000 and jointly agree not to accept any offer below $1,600,000.

Bottom lines, however, lack flexibility. By definition a bottom line is a fixed position which must not be changed, and once we mentally anchor ourselves to a bottom line, we shut our ears to new information which might cause us to change our position – up or down.

Bottom lines stifle creativity. There is no longer any incentive to create an imaginative solution which will optimise the value for both sides. Almost every negotiation involves more than one variable. Instead of selling the business for $1,600,000 you might serve your needs better by settling for $1,200,000, a guarantee of consultancy work from the new owners, and a royalty on all sales of a software package which you believe has immense potential. Bottom lines, because of their rigidity, block out imaginative solutions like these.

Also, bottom lines are often unrealistic. Buyers are notorious for setting unrealistic buying prices, while sellers commonly overvalue their goods.

BATNA

To overcome unrealistic, inflexible bottom lines, Harvard Professors Roger Fisher and William Ury coined the acronym BATNA – *the Best Alternative To a Negotiated Agreement*. A BATNA is a no-agreement standard used to judge any proposed agreement.

A BATNA involves three steps:

- First, you list everything you could do if you do not reach agreement.

Imagine you are working as an editor for a book publisher in a small country town and it's time again for you to negotiate your salary and benefits package. Your list of alternatives includes resigning and moving to a nearby city where there are four sizeable book publishers who publish in your field of expertise – technical publications. You could also leave publishing and move into a completely new career field.

- Second, you explore the best of your options and try to improve on them.

You ring local and out of town employment agencies to test out the demand for your book editing skills and apply for two positions. You also explore moving out of book editing. To test your assumptions about your chances of winning a job in another career field you redraft your CV and apply for three vacancies. To your delight you land a job offer as a technical editor with Sytech Books as well as a job with the local branch of Angus and Peterson Public Relations in client liaison work.

- Finally you choose the best option. This is your BATNA.

Your partner doesn't want to move towns so you decide your best option is to change careers and move into public relations. This is your BATNA.

Armed with a strong BATNA you can negotiate with confidence and power. On the other hand, if your BATNA is worse than you hoped, you should temper your demands.

It always pays to consider what the other party's BATNA is as well. What alternatives, for example, do your employers have? How easily could they replace you?

A BATNA thus shows you how to measure your proposals against *realistic* alternatives rather than rigid bottom lines. If you use a BATNA you will never negotiate blind, and the stronger your BATNA, the greater your bargaining power. If the other party's offers are better than your BATNA, take them; if the offers are worse, bargain to improve them.

If a negotiation is going badly, don't hesitate to reveal your BATNA to increase your leverage. However, you will only weaken your case if you reveal a BATNA that is worse than the other side already imagines.

If you deadlock you can always use your BATNA. A BATNA, after all, is your alternative to agreement – your walk away position.

Skilled negotiators work very hard to improve their BATNA.

Times are financially tough for Environmental Tours. Tourist numbers are down and the bank has just raised its interest rates. To reduce debt, Environmental Tours owner Kate Leggart decides to sell Eco-View, a specialist purpose-built boat designed for working in shallow wetlands. Alan Peck, who runs a similar business in a neighbouring region, offers $17,000 for the boat. Kate very nearly sells – but decides to check around.

The local boat dealer, Pylite Marine, says there is very little demand for specialist boats such as the Eco-View and offers $12,000.

Given this offer, Alan Peck's $17,000 offer suddenly looks much more attractive. Even so, it is still well below the $63,000 it would cost to replace Eco-View.

Price of the Boat

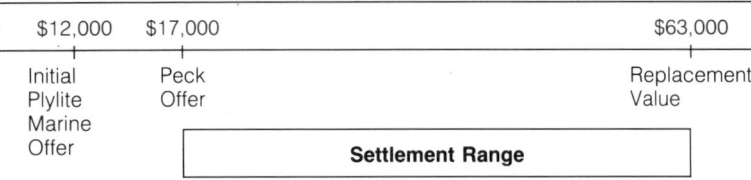

Price of the boat

Kate suddenly has a brainwave. The local university may want to buy Eco-View for its research programme. Unfortunately the university has no spare funds. But if Kate donates the boat she will receive a tax deduction for making a charitable donation of approximately $22,000.

By improving her BATNA, Kate raises her reserve price from $17,000 to $22,000. Armed with this information she calls up Alan Peck who, after a brief bargaining session, agrees to pay $24,500.

Look at how the Maltese Government improved their BATNA while simultaneously worsening the British Government's BATNA in their 1971 negotiations over renewed naval base rights.

During the Second World War the naval base at Malta had played a critical role in Britain's naval defence plans. By 1970, however, the Maltese bases were no longer of such importance because of improvements in ship design and changes in methods of warfare.

To raise the base rentals the Maltese openly courted the Soviet Union with a proposal to put a base in Malta. They also asked Libya and other Arab states for large assistance payments in exchange for Malta's neutrality.

These moves not only improved Malta's BATNA with the British, but the same moves simultaneously worsened Britain's BATNA. *The Times* of London noted, "What is important . . . is not that [the facilities] are badly needed in an age of nuclear war but they should not on the other hand be possessed by Russia."

As well as raising the pressure on Britain, the Maltese move raised concerns among Britain's NATO partners who, in turn, expressed their concerns to Britain.

As a result Britain increased its rental payments 400% while other NATO members provided additional aid to Malta. The Maltese improved their own BATNA, and at the same time worsened those of the others. The result: a much better deal for Malta.[4]

Listing Your Interests

The purpose of negotiating is to satisfy your interests. Interests are what motivate us and include our needs, desires, concerns, and fears.

Reconcile Interests

Too often in negotiations we forget that to settle our differences we have to reconcile our interests. Foolishly we concentrate on our positions.

Two sisters, Amy and Alicia, are quarrelling over the last orange in the fruit bowl. "It's mine," cries Amy. "But I have to have it," counters Alicia.

Enter Mother. "Enough of this arguing," she says as she grabs a knife and cuts the orange in two. "Here, half for you, Alicia, and half for you, Amy."

The 50-50 split seems as fair a solution as you can imagine. Yet when Mother checks on Amy a few moments later, she finds Amy has squeezed out the orange juice for a drink, while Alicia has used the peel of the orange in a cake she is baking.

This tale is typical of many negotiations where both sides take and defend a position. Unless one side is prepared to give in, the result is deadlock.

Yet if both sides had taken the time to dig behind their stated positions by questioning each other about their underlying interests, both could have had all they wanted. Amy could have had all the juice; Alicia, all of the peel.

It's easy to understand why negotiators too often focus on positions. Positions are usually obvious and easy to identify, whereas interests often seem vague, intangible and obscure.

Over 40 years ago, psychologist Abraham Maslow constructed a motivation model of human needs. Although it is by no means a complete explanation it is still useful in helping explain what motivates us.

Maslow identified five different categories of needs which he arranged in a hierarchy.

Basic Physical Needs. Our first need is for essentials such as food, clothing and shelter.

Safety Needs. After our basic needs are satisfied we then turn our attention to satisfying our need to make ourselves safe and secure from danger.

Social Needs. We all need to belong and satisfy our need for love, affection and affiliation.

Esteem Needs. As we progress up the needs hierarchy we want to be recognised by others – prestige, status, respect and fame are all intangible needs that are bestowed by others.

Self-Fulfilment. The ultimate need or motive that drives us is self-fulfilment or self-actualization.

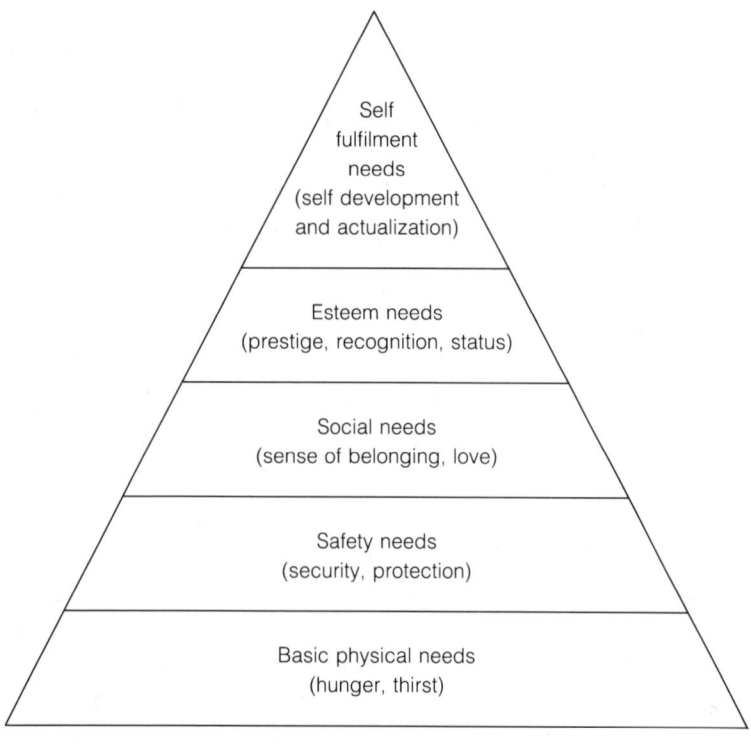

Maslow's hierarchy of needs

Michael Renz is one of Mercedes Benz of Germany's most successful sales staff. In two years he increased turnover in one of Germany's more difficult sales territories by 80%. On average he meets a customer five times before concluding a sale. During that time he continually probes prospects with questions to uncover their needs. He then matches up the buying motives of his prospects with Maslow's hierarchy of needs.

If they reveal a need for image or status, he matches it to their "esteem needs", and he pushes features such as deep rich colour, the metallic paint, the alloy wheels.

If they indicate a need for safety, he ties it to security. He then sells safety features such as the structure of the car and the airbag.[5]

Discovering needs is like gift buying. When you purchase gifts for close friends you can probably think of dozens of things they would be delighted to receive. Because you have an intimate understanding of their needs there are lots of ways you can meet their interests. Buying gifts for strangers is, of course, much more difficult.

One easy way out would be not to look for a gift at all. You could send them money. (That's what sales staff do all the time. When they can't be bothered discovering their customer's true needs, they simply cut the price.)

Another way would be to look at what other people are giving similar sorts of people and follow them. Both of these solutions are unsatisfactory. If you want to put together deals that last and are good for both sides, you have to take time to discover the other party's needs.

The year: 1955. The scene: The head office of an American retail chain. A young businessman, Akio Morita, from the Sony Corporation of Japan, is selling one of the world's first transistor radios.

The buyer is enthusiastic. "Can you give me a price on 5000, 10,000, 30,000, 50,000 and 100,000 radios?" he asks.

Akio Morita returns the next day with the price. The buyer stares at the quote in amazement. He can't believe his eyes. He puts down the paper and patiently says, "Mr Morita, I have been working as a purchasing agent for nearly 30 years, and you are the first person who has ever come in here and told me the more I buy the higher the unit price will be. It's illogical!"

Akio Morita explains. "At the moment we do not have the capacity to produce 100,000 radios. If we accept your order for 100,000, we will have to greatly expand capacity. It would need a giant investment. It's a gamble. And if we don't get a repeat order next year we will be in big trouble – perhaps bankrupt. I'm only prepared to take a huge order if we make enough profit on it to pay for all the new facilities we will need during the life of the order. In Japan we cannot just hire people and fire people whenever our orders go up or down. We are committed to our employees long term, as they are to us."

When the buyer gets over his shock, he smiles and orders ten thousand radios at the ten thousand unit price. Never again will he assume all sellers have the *same interests*.[6]

Identifying the Interests of the Other Party

If you are honest with yourself, you shouldn't have much trouble identifying your own interests. Uncovering your opponent's needs requires more imagination and skill.

To identify the interests of the other party, you need to be able to put yourself inside your counterpart's head. You need to be able to empathise – or as the Sioux Indians say "walk in your neighbour's moccasins".

To identify your opponent's interests, examine each position they take and ask "why?" Imagine you are the agent for Christina Petros, an up and coming opera singer. The local opera company want her to take the lead role but claim they can only afford $28,000, significantly below your normal base fee of $42,000 for a production of this type. You know their last production was a financial disaster and they can't afford to suffer another similar loss. You therefore say you will accept $28,000 as a base fee so long as they pay a royalty for each seat filled above 75% capacity. If the entire season is a sell out Christina will earn $65,000. The opera company agrees.

Another way to uncover interests is to list each of the points you want the other side to agree to. Then ask yourself what might stop the other side agreeing to your requests. The answers you come up with will very likely include their interests.

Listing, Ranking and Valuing the Issues

List the Issues

Once you have identified your interests, you can start drawing up your objectives.

To turn your interests into concrete objectives, ask yourself: If the other side agrees with me, what exactly do I want them to do?

If you were negotiating a salary and benefits package, you might say to yourself: "A salary of $65,000 a year would satisfy my interest in being paid what I feel I am worth. A five-year contract of employment plus a lump sum severance payment of $95,000 when I finish will satisfy my interest in receiving adequate job security." The salary, the contract of employment and the severance payment are the issues which will be negotiated.

When preparing for a negotiation, draw up a list of as many possible issues as you can. Professional negotiators always try to multiply the number of possible issues for negotiation. The more issues there are, the more tradables there are to create a package which will satisfy the other party's needs.

Amateur negotiators often try to simplify matters by concentrating on a few issues. Unfortunately, the fewer the issues, the more difficult it is to create a win-win settlement. In a single issue negotiation – say, over the price of a car – whenever the other party advances you have to retreat. It's classic win-lose. If, on the other hand, you increase the issues, you also multiply the variables and increase the possible ways you can negotiate a package which is good for both sides.

Rank Your Issues

Negotiation implies you are prepared to give as well as to take. It is unlikely that you will achieve all of your aims so you will have to concede on certain issues in order to achieve other ones.

It follows, therefore, that you should know clearly which issues are of vital importance and which you are prepared to concede.

Rank your issues into three groups:

High Priority. Of top priority are your *must gets*. These are your essentials. If you don't achieve these you will walk away from the negotiation table.

Medium Priority. Of moderate priority are your *should gets*. You expect to achieve these. Indeed you will be very disappointed if you don't achieve most of them.

Low Priority. Of lowest priority are your *could gets*. You would like to achieve these but they are the issues you are prepared to concede on in order to achieve your must gets.

Value Every Issue

Professional negotiators know what every issue under negotiation is worth. If they are negotiating a computer system, they know exactly what it costs to concede free delivery, weekend installation, extra documentation and extended credit. As they prepare, they measure the cost of every variable. They never forget to ask what it's worth.

Virtually any item in a business negotiation can be reduced to an objective monetary value. Watch your accountant value the goodwill in a business you intend selling, and you quickly see the benefits of putting a monetary value on even intangible issues.

After valuing what each issue is worth to you, ask "What is each one worth to the other party?"

The differences between how you and the other party value the issues provide the basis for successful negotiations. The essence of good bargaining is to trade goods that are inexpensive for you to concede but are valuable to the other party.

Determining the Other Side's Objectives

Once you've listed your own objectives, do the same for the other party.

This will help you answer three critical questions:

- What do they really want?

- How far can they go on each issue? (What are their limits?)
- What are their priorities?

This exercise is always difficult and involves lots of speculation. Assessing the other party's priorities is as difficult as assessing their maximum limits. Nevertheless, it is of critical importance and you'll be amazed how often analyzing the negotiation from the other side's perspective yields invaluable insights.

Compare Priorities

Once you've worked out their priorities you can now compare their priorities to yours. Every difference provides a potential trading opportunity, and once you have them, you're ready to draw up a list of possible trades.

Gathering Valuable Information

As Sales Manager of Matrex Electronics, Tim Levitt was concerned about the large number of bids for assembly work they were missing out on. To find out what was going on, he asked all of the sales staff to collect as much information as they could on their competitors before tendering any proposals. They gathered information from past sales reports, analyzed their competitors' annual reports and gathered data on their competitors' products at local trade shows. They even bought samples of their competitors' products and pulled them apart. Having collected as much information as they could, they assembled their proposal.

The results: Previously, where no competitor information had been gathered, the sales staff won only 37% of the bids. However in bids that used competitor information, the sales staff won 83% of their bids.

Knowledge is power in negotiation. The party with the most information will usually end up with the best deal. Sometimes we forget that negotiations exist only because of a lack of information. If, for instance, you knew in advance what the minimum was that your landlord would accept as a rental for his property, you could open at his limit position and refuse to budge. Hence there would be no point in negotiating.

Incomplete information is, therefore, the rule, not the exception in negotiations.

When preparing, ask:

What information do we already have?
Experienced negotiators continually gather information on their opponents. Annual reports, newspaper clippings, notes on past dealings, etc, should all be filed.

What extra information do we need?
If you are buying personal computers from a supplier, you will need competitors' prices, discounts, and so on.

Where and from whom can we gather it?
Intelligence gathering requires an agile mind and lots of gall. The party you are about to bargain with is not likely to tell you their production costs. However, there may be lots of people around who have worked in the same industry and who are only too happy to share their expertise. If you are worried about a potential supplier's ability to meet deadlines, ring some of their other customers. Most will readily share their experiences. Don't ignore obvious sources such as the Trade Directories and Business Who's Who.

The copier division of the Xerox Corporation has developed an elaborate intelligence gathering operation to monitor its competitors.

Staff start out thoroughly reviewing the patent literature. In Xerox's lab, they pull apart competitors' machines and calculate the cost of making each part.

To monitor Kodak's distribution and handling costs, Xerox purchase Kodak copiers, track where they were sent from and scrutinise the packaging. Engineers then assess how it is installed, how long it takes to set up and what tools are needed. They even buy a Kodak service contract so they can watch their competitors' service team in action.[7]

Information is especially powerful when you are negotiating with a number of suppliers or customers. You should gather as much data as you can from every potential supplier and customer. Then list the best each has to offer.

When you get down to bargaining, you can say, "Peter Jones at Bendrill Machines has offered 22.5% discount and 60 days to pay ... Joe Johnson at Winkler Services has offered a warranty that covers both parts and labour for two years instead of the one that you are offering." Specific facts and figures such as these give you considerable leverage.

How to Gather
Business Intelligence

In the business sector more and more companies are systematically gathering intelligence. Here are some tips on where to inexpensively gather data.

Databases: Thousands of databases exist containing articles from newspapers, magazines, trade directories, stock analyst's reports and other sources.

Specialty Trade Magazines: Trade magazines include announcements such as personnel shifts, new product announcements and times of trade conferences.

News Clippings: Newspaper clipping services will collect information on virtually any topic.

Market Research Studies: Virtually every industry publishes market research reports.

Stock Analyst Reports: If you want information on an organisation that is part of a publicly traded company, check out stock analyst reports.

Trade Conferences: Trade shows are great sources of product literature and other industry related information.

Public Records: All companies must file documents to comply with various laws. Some of these documents contain sensitive information.

Advertisements: Published advertising expenditure figures on competitors' products will often provide clues to their marketing strategies.

Job Vacancies: Situations vacant advertisements often give away lots of useful information in their attempts to sell prospective employees on a career.

Personal Contacts: Build up a file of useful contacts in the industry you are operating in. Consultants and employees of industry sector groups will often provide invaluable information.

Source: Leonard M. Fuld, *Monitoring the Competition, Find Out What's Really Going On Over There*, John Wiley & Sons, New York 1988.

Analysing the Other Party

Before President Sadat of Egypt and Prime Minister Begin of Israel arrived at Camp David in September 1978 for critical Middle East peace talks, American President Jimmy Carter had detailed biographies prepared on the two adversaries.

The thick psychological analyses delved into every aspect of the two men's lives. They analysed: "What had made them [Sadat and Begin] national leaders? What was the root of their ambition? What were their most important goals in life . . .? Likely reaction to intense pressure in time of crisis? Strengths and weaknesses? . . . Whom did they *really* trust? What was their attitude towards one another?"[8]

Jimmy Carter wanted to know exactly what made Sadat and Begin tick. For 13 days Carter used the insights derived from this intelligence to keep the two enemies talking while nudging them towards an historic accord.

When facing a negotiator across the table, we need to be aware that sometimes the needs of the other negotiators are not the same as the organisation they represent.

Consider: Anne Silvester, Top Tier Flooring salesperson, needs just $78,000 of sales in the next three days to reach her annual sales quota of $800,000 for the calendar year. If she reaches her sales goal, she will receive a three week, all expenses paid, Mediterranean holiday.

The customer, Vincent Architects, is planning to put in new flooring in the new year. So to push forward the sale, Anne offers a 22.5% discount.

When Anne's boss hears about the sale she berates Anne. "Why did you offer a discount?" she declares. "Our manufacturing operation is already at full capacity. We have a three week lead time already."

At the root of the problem are the differing needs of Anne and the company she works for. A skilled negotiator will uncover these different sets of needs and turn them to advantage.

Rehearsing by Role Playing

A valuable preparation technique is to simulate an impending negotiation by role-playing. Ask a colleague to help you stage a mock negotiation. You can ask the colleague to role play your opponent. In playing your opponent, she should expose any weaknesses in your plan.

Often it is more useful for you to take the part of your opponent. The insights you gain into your opponent's interests should prove invaluable when you plan your negotiating strategy. One of the best ways to *inoculate* yourself against being too influenced by the arguments of the other side is to prepare counter arguments against your own case.

When choosing an opponent to role play a negotiation with, try to get someone who performs the same function as the person you will actually be bargaining with. For example, if you are a seller, ask someone from purchasing to play the buyer.

If you can, video the role play. Everyone benefits from seeing themself in video playback. The standard of analysis rises, as the nature of playback means you can analyse the events in the sequence they actually occurred.

Testing Your Assumptions

It was the end of season for the 4H Farm Club. Most of the kids were auctioning off their pet sheep which they had raised from lambs.

One tearful girl seemed particularly upset by the sale. The higher the bidding for her sheep went, the more she cried.

Finally a wealthy rancher intervened, bid $1000, won the auction and in a grand public gesture donated the sheep back to the weeping girl.

Several months later the same rancher found himself judging an essay contest at the local school. And one of the submissions was from the same little girl. One crucial passage described the auction.

"The higher they bid for my sheep," she wrote, "the happier I became. I was so happy I was crying. The happier I got the more I cried. Finally my sheep sold for $1000, and the man who paid more than I ever dreamed possible gave my sheep back to me.

"When I got home my dad barbecued it. It was really delicious."[9]

When you don't have all the information, you're forced to make assumptions. We all make assumptions. We have to. When you negotiate with someone old, you may automatically assume they are conservative. You negotiate with a Sunday School teacher, and you assume they are honest. And so it goes on. Beware! Never treat your assumptions as facts.

As you go through your assumptions, write down on paper all the questions you need to ask to verify them. Don't rely on your memory. It's too easy to forget.

When you meet face to face ask questions such as:

- Am I correct in assuming you will want early delivery now that you are reorganising your assembly line?
- If you and I agree today, can I presume you have full authority to commit your organisation?

• Am I correct in assuming quality is the main stumbling block at the moment?

Consulting With Others

If you represent a group or organisation, you must consult with those whom you represent. A negotiator who bargains on behalf of others and who sets the issues on the agenda without consultation is inviting trouble.

You would be a brave person if you bought a house without consulting your spouse. Unions which don't consult their members can end up humiliated when their membership rejects the proposed settlement out of hand. Failure to consult leads to the ignoring of important concerns and misunderstandings over priorities.

Often negotiators will discover their constituency's "want list" is unrealistic. Negotiators then have to separately negotiate with their constituency over the content of the agenda.

Determining the Limit of Your Authority

If you negotiate on behalf of somebody else, you will need to meet with them to set the limits of your authority to negotiate each issue. This is essential. If you ever make a deal and your principal reneges, your credibility soon evaporates.

Negotiators who are unsure about their authority are in a weak position. If you know your limit, you are more commanding and assertive, and the confidence that you gain from knowing you will be backed up will strengthen your position.

Never admit during a negotiation to having total authority to make an agreement. It is always handy to be able to retreat from a difficult spot by saying, "this is subject to board approval." If your opponent puts you on the spot and asks, "Can you finalise the deal?" reply, "Yes, if it is within the limits set by my principal."

Union negotiators often claim they must refer the agreement back to the membership for final approval. When faced with a situation such as this, test the negotiator's personal commitment. Propose: "Will you personally recommend what we have agreed, if we will make a final offer which includes your demands on sick leave."

Sometimes negotiators use limited authority as a tactic to secure extra concessions. They assure you ratification is a mere formality then return saying their principal requires further concessions. To protect yourself against this ruse, hold back some concessions which you can offer as a final sweetener to secure agreement.

Authority levels are not always obvious. Don't assume from a company or government organisation chart you know who the "monkeys" and the "organ grinders" are. Before you start bargaining there are usually opportunities to ask:

- How do you go about making decisions such as this?
- Who gets involved in making these decisions?
- How much time do decisions such as these usually take?

Planning Your Agenda
List and Order the Issues
You are now ready to plan your agenda. An agenda should list the issues that you want to discuss, in the order you want to negotiate them.

When you have lots of issues to negotiate, start with the minor issues first. Imagine facing a tough opponent who is out to fleece you. If you start with the minor issues, you get the chance to invent creative solutions and build rapport. Discussing easier issues first may also reveal extra variables. These are often useful tradables if you later stall over a critical issue.

Some negotiators prefer to start with the toughest issues. They claim everyone's fresher and usually in a more constructive mind at the beginning of the session. Still others prefer to block issues into logical chunks. Whatever pattern you choose, make sure it is consistent with your strategy.

When planning your agenda remember to note the issues that you want to avoid. Don't undermine your chances by raising issues you are weak in. For example, if you are negotiating a proposal for the supply of colour plastic laminates, there is no point in raising the colours your range lacks.

Written agendas can be sent to the other side for comment and revision. This builds goodwill and you'll be surprised how often people agree to follow your agenda without any changes.

Alternatively, your agenda plan can remain private to you – hidden from the other party. If they haven't prepared an agenda, you will have the advantage of being able to control the flow of bargaining.

Never underrate the importance of agenda setting. Diplomats spend days, even weeks, over agendas. Business negotiators, to their cost, rarely give them the thought they deserve.

Planning Your Critical First Offer

At the turn of the century American steel magnate Andrew Carnegie sold his steel interests for $300 million to fellow financial titan, J.P. Morgan. There was no negotiation. Carnegie, who never bargained, simply jotted his price on a piece of paper, handed it to an intermediary, who in turn passed it on to Morgan. Glancing at the paper, Morgan mumbled, "I accept".

Years later, legend has it that the two millionaires bumped into each other on the promenade deck of an Atlantic liner. "I have been thinking," said Carnegie, "that I should have asked you for $500 million." "I would have paid it," replied Morgan – and walked away.

Before you start bargaining, you need to calculate what you are initially going to offer. More than any other single factor, your first offer will shape the outcome of the final deal, so it's vital to plan it carefully.

As a buyer, should you start low and take an extreme position, or should you start high to create a more co-operative stance? An experiment carried out by UCLA psychologists examined this question.

Some 140 pairs of negotiators were given a sum of money to bargain over. For the purpose of this example let's make it $35. They were told that if they could agree on how to divide the money they could keep it, but if they didn't reach agreement in the allotted time neither would get it.

On one side of the negotiation tables were volunteers who thought they were participating in a straight test of bargaining skills. Unknown to them, on the other side were experimenters under instructions to bargain in one of three ways.

With one group, the experimenters opened with a high demand of $30, then gradually retreated in steps to $25 then $20.

With a second group of subjects, the experimenters opened with a high initial demand of $30 and then reso-lutely stuck to that demand throughout the negotiation.

With a third group, the experimenters opened with a moderate demand of $20 and then steadfastly refused to budge from their opening position.

The psychologists found:

1.   The strategy of starting with a high demand then steadily retreating to a more moderate one produced the most money for the negotiators using it.

2.   The group facing the negotiators who used the retreating strategy felt they had successfully influenced the deal much more than the other two groups. They believed their persuasion skills had induced the concessions, and felt more responsible for the final outcome of the nego- tiations. It seems a person who feels they have helped shape a deal will be more likely to live up to the terms.

3.   Even though they gave away the most money, the victims of the concessions strategy were the most satisfied with the final split. Agreements forged by the give and take of mutual con- cessions satisfy an important psychological need.

This experiment, and other similar research studies, confirms what generations of experienced negotiators have claimed:

• Buyers do better when they start with a low offer.
• Sellers do better when they start high.

Not only does it give you more room to make concessions but also the other party seem to gauge their success by the size of the concessions they extract.

When you aim high, however, you increase the risk of rejection. An opening offer should therefore always be realistic and credible. Of course, what is realistic and credible depends on the circumstances. If you are buying second-hand furniture, an opening offer of 50 percent below the asking figure might be realistic. A similar offer for a house will normally be rejected as ridiculous. If you can't justify your initial offer with logic and reason, don't use it.

Picking a Winning Team

Some negotiators prefer negotiating alone. They like the extra control it gives and they complain that teams are unwieldy, too unpredictable. Teams sometimes fragment, members contradict each other, leak information and give away unauthorised concessions. Teams deadlock more often and take much longer to reach agreement.

Nevertheless a well organised, well led team is difficult to beat. Even the simplest negotiation is complex. It's rare to find a negotiator who can talk, listen, watch, think and plan at the same time. These are tasks that need sharing. When it comes to analysing the mass of facts and technical data that often passes across the negotiation table, two or more heads cope better than one.

Team negotiations allow multiple interests to be represented. Participation builds commitment to the final agreement. An effective team raises the confidence and assertiveness of all its members and a well managed team is a formidable opponent.

Teams must be disciplined and well organised. Specific functions should be allocated to different team members. Ideally a *leader, reviewer, observer* and *analyst* should be appointed to take on the four key tasks.

Leader. The team leader handles all the face-to-face bargaining. The leader orchestrates the play, does most of the talking, raises new issues, makes proposals and trades concessions.

Reviewer. Because of the demands of leading, the leader sometimes gets sidetracked or simply needs a break. When this happens the reviewer takes over. The reviewer summarises the progress to date and clarifies points with questions. By summarising and clarifying, the reviewer builds momentum and creates breathing space for the leader. The reviewer, however, should never raise new issues or trade concessions. This quickly undermines the leader's authority.

Observer. A third team member should play the role of observer. The observer focuses on the verbal and non-verbal messages to try to understand the other side's objectives, priorities and concerns.

Analyst. The fourth team member, the analyst, records and analyses all the numbers and other data.

Teams should take regular breaks for private discussion. During recess the leader will use information from the observer and analyst, and other team members, to plan the next session.

The observer and analyst should always be on the lookout for patterns. The pattern of offers and concessions invariably offers insights to the other side's objectives and priorities.

A sale for a four million dollar manufacturing assembly system was under negotiation. The leader for the sales team felt well satisfied with the morning session. The buyer had conceded on a number of important points. However during the recess discussions, the analyst's notes showed the buyer had made two concessions on price, one on service, yet had refused to budge on the deposit and scheduling of the repayments.

The observer had noticed the buyer seemed to be avoiding eye contact and was distinctly hesitant whenever repayments came up in the discussion. All the signs suggested repayment terms were a priority for the buyer. Was cashflow a problem? And if so, how big a problem?

A check with headquarters revealed that one of the buyer's major customers had just folded with a string of unpaid debts. Perhaps the buyer had been caught too.

Armed with this information the leader prepared for the afternoon session. Cashflow was indeed a problem. The buyer had been burnt by the company collapse, but had sufficient forward orders to see them through the crisis. They would have liked to defer the assembly purchase, but they couldn't fulfil the orders on time without it. Eventually the seller agreed to a low deposit and extended terms in return for personal guarantees for the money from two of the major shareholders.

In a team of three the analyst should also play observer. In a duo the reviewer bears the extra burden of observing and analyzing.

If you need experts and specialists, make sure they are well briefed and instructed not to get caught up in long winded debate with their opposite number. Technical experts can easily undermine a negotiating stance with effusive displays of knowledge. Specialists must be made aware that the leader calls the tune and may choose to ignore technical expertise. If you anticipate problems with your experts, send them on a negotiation training course.

Sometimes in labour negotiations one side will try to gain an advantage by outnumbering the opposition. Numbers, however, can only intimidate if you let them. A small, well trained team is usually more than a match for a cumbersome opponent.

Devising a Time Plan

Time in negotiations is the great pressuriser; the way we use it is crucial to success in a negotiation.

During the 1968 Paris-Vietnam Peace Talks, US negotiator Averill Harriman was sent to Paris by President Lyndon Johnson. It was election year and President Johnson wanted a quick resolution to the problem.

In Paris, Harriman rented an hotel room on a week-to-week basis.

The North Vietnamese leased a villa for two-and-a-half years. They then proceeded to spend week after week arguing over the shape of the negotiating table.

After 30 years of fighting, the North Vietnamese were prepared to take their time to get what they wanted.

Deadlines

Both sides in a negotiation operate under deadline pressure. Most concessions and settlements occur at or near the deadline. If you have to get the components by Wednesday, your demands soften on Tuesday. If you have to seal the deal by Good Friday, you make your biggest concessions on Easter Thursday. If you have to catch a plane to be home for the weekend, your bargaining power crumbles as you contemplate a long weekend in a miserable hotel.

Back in 1973, property developer Donald Trump's ambition to purchase the monster 1400 room Commodore Hotel in central New York seemed little more than a fanciful idea. Yet over the next three years Trump stitched together a viable package. First, in late 1974 he obtained an option for a paltry $250,000 from the financially troubled owners to purchase the hotel. Then Trump signed up Hyatt Hotels as hotel operator and equal partner – subject to finance and a deal with New York City to abate property taxes. After extensive lobbying, the city agreed to abate tens of millions of dollars of property taxes over 40 years. Finally, Equitable Life Assurance Society agreed to lend $35 million and Bowery Savings Bank $45 million to finance the deal.

Thus it seemed little more than a formality when Trump, the Bank and Hyatt met to sign the papers that would conclude the deal. Then Trump played his wild card. He privately told the bank that theirs was a risky investment and to protect it they should insist on a restrictive covenant from Hyatt to prohibit them building further hotels in New York without Trump's permission. With the covenant in place, Hyatt wouldn't be able to build another hotel close by and so threaten its viability.

Taking Trump's bait, the banker stormed into the room where the Hyatt people were waiting. "Hey fellahs," he said, "we're putting up tens of millions of dollars, which is a lot of money, and we're not going to make this loan unless we get a covenant from Hyatt saying you won't open up any other hotels in New York."[10]

It was an extraordinary risk for Trump to take. Then and there the financing, and with it the deal, could have collapsed. But Trump knew Jay Pritzker, the head of the Hyatt Group, who had already rejected Trump's proposal for a covenant at an earlier meeting, was away mountain climbing in Nepal and couldn't be reached.

The bank gave Hyatt one hour to make a decision. Meanwhile Trump drew up the terms of the covenant. In effect, it prohibited Hyatt from opening any competing hotels in the New York area. The only exception was the right to build a small luxury hotel, which would be economically unfeasible anyway. Before the hour was up, Hyatt signed the covenant.

Trump got his hotel and a potentially even more valuable right that allowed him to control the expansion plans of a possible competitor.

Deadlines, as Trump knew, cause negotiators to soften their demands. When negotiators are under time pressure, they lower their aspirations, bluff less frequently and make more concessions.

Deadlines increase the pressure to reach agreement. Bargainers change their position more rapidly when under time pressure.

Knowing your opponent's deadline will give you an edge. So don't reveal your deadlines to the other side unless you have to. To counter deadline pressure prepare a time plan. Anticipate what you will do if the negotiation drags, and prepare for evasive action. If you find yourself in a deadline trap, ask:

- Is there any way I can extend my own deadline?
- What can I do to alter the deadline pressures being used by the other party?

Remember, most deadlines are the result of negotiations, so they may well be negotiable.

Be Patient

To counter deadline pressure, remain calm and cool, and display great patience. Act as though there is plenty of time available. Whenever you feel as though you're about to buckle under time pressure, remember: the negotiations that ended the Korean War took two years and 575 meetings; the Austrian State Treaty negotiations stretched over eight years and 400 meetings.

Having enough time to decide can make the difference between peace and war. George Ball, one of President Kennedy's senior advisors during the Cuban missile crisis, reports that when he and his fellow advisors met again, many years later, "much to our own surprise, we reached the unanimous opinion that, had we determined our course of action within the first 48 hours after the [Russian] missiles were discovered [on Cuba], we would have almost certainly made the wrong decision, responding to the missiles in such a way as to require a forceful Soviet response and thus setting in train a series of reactions and counter-reactions with horrendous consequences."[11]

Use a Time Plan

Anticipate what you will do if a negotiation drags out and prepare accordingly. In other words, make time work for you.

Use deadlines to create momentum. If a deadline doesn't exist, create one, for example:

- The purchasing committee meets on Thursday. Could you have the specifications to me by midday Wednesday.
- The freighter leaves on the 22nd. Do you want us to book space on it?

If you suffer from a deadline disadvantage, create incentives for a quick agreement. Sellers everywhere use variations of these two:

- The first three buyers to buy a new Ford today get three years free servicing.

- For this month only we are offering a free spreadsheet package and a laser printer with every networked system purchased.

Avoiding the Time Trap

Deadlines are not the only time pressure you have to cope with. The more time you invest in a negotiation, the more committed you become to a deal and the more you have to lose if the deal turns sour. As your time investment increases, the more vulnerable you become to a claim for additional concessions in the closing stages of a deal.

To protect yourself from time entrapment:

1. Fix a date for the completion of the negotiations beyond which you will not go. Make it clear to your opponent that you will break off negotiations if negotiations are not complete by the deadline.

2. Treat last-minute demands for additional concessions as a chance for you to call for a re-examination of all the other issues already negotiated. Most times your opponent will drop the "add-ons". If not, you can renegotiate other parts of the larger package to compensate for the late requests.

Sometimes it is better to walk away from a deal. We praise negotiators for the good deals they conclude. We should also thank them for the bad ones they avoid. British Prime Minister Neville Chamberlain will always be remembered for the Munich Agreement – which handed over the Sudaten territory of Czechoslovakia to Hitler without a fight in 1938. Sir Samuel Hoare, who was a member of the British cabinet during the negotiations with Hitler, confessed later,

"The longer it went on and the more serious it became, the more anxious I grew to see it succeed."[12]

Deals rarely get worse when you walk away from the table. Usually when you return you find you can negotiate even better terms.

Choosing a Venue

Where should you negotiate? At your premises? At your client's place? Or should you travel to neutral territory?

Each venue has its advantages.

Sports teams like playing at home. It's much harder to win away. Only one first division English football team, Liverpool, was able to win more away games than it lost in the 1980s.

Experiments show negotiators are more assertive at home. You feel more comfortable. You can easily access your data and experts. You schedule the coffee breaks, control the physical arrangements and interruptions, and you can use time as a pressuriser.

The home advantage is even more apparent in international negotiations. Outsiders are expected to follow local customs and norms, and on someone else's territory you are on unfamiliar ground. As a guest you are expected to behave more correctly. Travelling to negotiations can also be tiring.

An away venue is not necessarily a disadvantage. Negotiators cannot walk out of their own building. They cannot say, "I'll have to check back at head office on that one." If they claim insufficient authority, you can ask, "Why not get your boss to join us." You can even ask for a tour of your opponent's premises.

A neutral location can prove very useful. You're away from the normal interruptions of the office. Fresh surroundings facilitate a fresh look at an intractable problem. When American President, Jimmy Carter, persuaded Israel's Prime Minister, Menachim Begin, and Egypt's President, Anwar Sadat, to journey to the secluded tranquil environment of Camp David for 13 days of Middle East peace talks in 1978, he insulated them from the daily hassles of government and the unrelenting scrutiny of the world's media.

The ultimate negotiation venue may be Panmunjom where the peace talks to end the Korean war were held. There, the peace talks building, and even the negotiating table, straddled the 38th parallel that divides North and South Korea. Each side entered the building from its own country and sat in its own territory during negotiations. Panmunjom had the same symbolic significance as a neutral country.

Physical Surroundings

Whatever the venue, don't neglect the physical surroundings. A spacious, airy, well ventilated, well lit negotiation room is essential. Avoid claustrophobic windowless rooms. Make sure the furniture is comfortable. Arrange separate recess rooms for team negotiations, with their own direct dial telephone, and access to facsimile and telex. And don't forget to have the room cleaned and tidied, and refreshments topped up during breaks.

Designing a Strategy: Choosing the Right Tactics

Your strategy is the gameplan you adopt to achieve your objectives. Within that, you choose specific tactics in order to achieve your strategy.

The strategy you adopt depends upon the type of nego-tiation. Before you can plan an effective strategy however, you first need to understand the dynamics of the complete negotiation process. Strategy and tactics are, therefore, dealt with separately in Chapters 13 and 14. For now, remember the best strategy is one that leaves both sides satisfied.

Step One: Ready Yourself

Checkpoints:

- Develop a BATNA.

- Identify your interests.

- Identify your opponent's interests.

- List, rank and value the issues.

- Gather information.

- Analyse the other party.

- Role play.

- Test your assumptions.

- Consult with others.

- Determine the limits of your authority.

- Plan your agenda.

- Determine your first offer.

- Choose your team members.

- Devise a time plan.

- Choose a venue.

- Plan your strategy.

- Choose appropriate tactics.

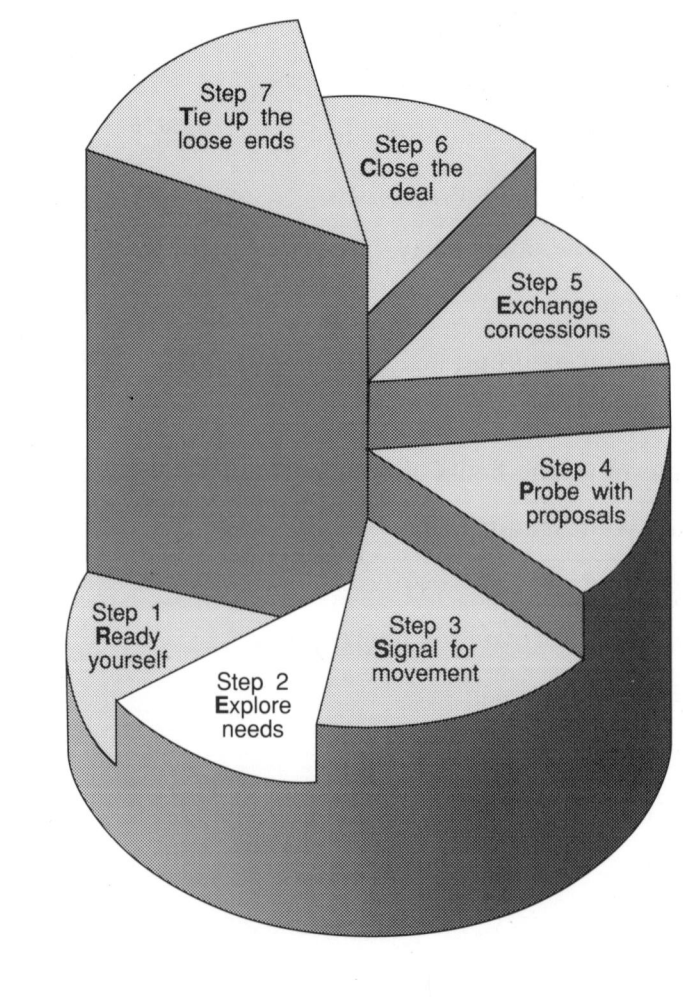

R-E-S-P-E-C-T
The seven steps to agreement

Step 7 Tie up the loose ends

Step 6 Close the deal

Step 5 Exchange concessions

Step 4 Probe with proposals

Step 3 Signal for movement

Step 2 Explore needs

Step 1 Ready yourself

CHAPTER FIVE

Step Two: Exploring Each Other's Needs

> *"I know you believe you*
> *understand what you think I think I said, but*
> *I'm not sure you realize that what you heard is*
> *not what I meant."*
>
> *Anon*

Having prepared, you're ready to meet the other side in face-to-face discussions to explore their needs. Ninety percent of the time in a typical negotiation we spend discussing – talking, listening and watching each other – and discovering each other's needs. How we discuss is, therefore, of vital importance.

The opening discussions set the tone and climate for the rest of the negotiation. You also disclose your opening position and discover the other side's position as well.

Setting the Tone and Climate

Destructive negotiators quickly sour the atmosphere by adopting aggressive postures. They threaten, blame, inter-rupt and even question the authority of the other party. As a result the temperature rises and the discussion degenerates into a point-scoring exercise. Destructive negotiators don't care about the needs of the other side. For them negotiation is a contest where there is only one winner.

Constructive negotiators, on the other hand, keep their cool. They calmly but firmly state their position and support it with reason and logic. They work hard to create a working relationship with the other party using questions and active listening to explore their needs. For them a negotiation should satisfy the needs of both sides. There doesn't have to be a loser; both sides can win.

Communicating Your Position

The opening positions of both sides set the parameters of the bargaining range, so how you open is crucial. If you've done your homework, you will have prepared an ambitious yet credible proposal. If new information emerges during discussions that shows your initial expectations were unrealistic, change your position now. Ridiculous opening stands are one of the great destroyers of credibility.

Keep your opening proposals brief and to the point. Don't provide too many details, or you may find them used against you in their counter-proposal.

Imagine you have just submitted a proposal to produce a monthly magazine for a client. Your total price of $72,000 is $13,000 less than your closest competitor, but your estimate for printing costs is $5000 higher. By providing your client with an unnecessarily detailed breakdown of your charges you have given her the information she needs to get you to shave your printing costs to the level of the competition.

When you present your opening position look the other person straight in the eye. Speak clearly and slowly with a confident, assured voice and act as though you expect your offer to be accepted. Avoid vague, tentative phrases such as:

- We would like to get *about* $50,000 for the section.

- We are looking for a price in *the range of* $25,000 to $30,000.
- For a *first offer* we are prepared to offer $26,000.

Offers such as these imply you're not serious and that you're a long way away from what you're prepared to settle for.

After you have stated your position, go quiet and wait for their reaction. Don't ask, "What do you think of my offer?" You're simply inviting rebuff and rejection. You're also implying you have some doubts as well.

Discovering Their Position

If possible get the other side to make the first offer. Most people provide far more information than they need to. They sometimes reveal their priorities, and every now and again they offer more than you ever dreamed of asking for.

If the other side makes the first offer, don't immediately make a counter offer. When is someone most committed to their position? Just after they've presented it, so wait instead for a more opportune moment. This will normally be after questioning has forced them to acknowledge some weaknesses in their opening position.

The Power of Questions

"Asking a question is like sharpening a pencil: Each apt question . . . whittles down the problem."

Gerald I. Nierenberg

Questions are the most potent communication tool a negotiator can use. All negotiators must know how and when to ask questions and use them to control the direction and pace of a negotiation.

Neil Rackham of the Huthwaite Research Group and John Carlisle observed hundreds of negotiators in action to discover what it takes to become a top negotiator. A key finding: "skilled negotiators ask more than twice as many questions as average negotiators."[13]

Questions Elicit Answers

Russian novelist Leo Tolstoy wrote, "There is no such thing as a right answer, only good and bad questions."

Most of us love answering questions. A large part of our schooling consists of learning how to answer questions. A question triggers an automatic response inside us; when we hear a question we feel an urge to answer.

We look down on those who avoid or can't answer questions. Watch how uncomfortable a politician appears when he answers "no comment" to a reporter's question. Negotiators who face their counterpart with a list of well thought out questions, therefore, always start with an advantage.

Questions Uncover Information

The most common use of questions is to gather information. The party with the best information in a negotiation always has an advantage. Before you start making offers of any kind, you need to fill in as many gaps in your knowledge as you can. Often the easiest way to get to the bottom of problems and uncover hidden information is to ask questions.

I was about to take over the lease of a suite of offices and warehouse. I had negotiated the lease with the landlord but still had to negotiate a price for the partitioning and other fittings the previous tenant had installed. The previous tenant had indicated by facsimile they were looking for $15,000.

The meeting took place at the previous tenant's new office. Wanda, my Promotions Manager who had done most of our homework for the negotiation, was also there in support.

For my first question I asked, "Could you please explain how you arrived at a price of $15,000?"

"I'm not really sure," replied the previous tenant's representative. "Our head office Financial Accountant set the figure. I gather he wants one-third for the partitioning we installed, one-third for the extra lighting we fitted and one-third for the carpeting we laid at our expense."

I replied, "Well we have no need for the carpet, we want to put in all new flooring to go with our new colour scheme. Our landlord has provided us with a plan of the original light fittings and from what we can work out, the only change you've made to the lighting is to install one extra fluorescent light. By my calculations that must have cost between $70 and $100 to install."

To add credence to the last point, Wanda pulled out of her briefcase a copy of the plans of the premises provided to us by the landlord and pointed out just where the extra light had gone in.

The other party was obviously unprepared. They'd assumed wrongly we wanted the carpet and had based their price on it. Their claim for the lighting was obviously ridiculous. So it wasn't surprising that after a little more discussion their asking price dropped to $5000.

Thirty minutes into the negotiation, my counterpart asked his first question. "What are you prepared to pay?"

I replied, "We're certainly interested in the partitioning, but for it to meet our needs we'll have to get carpenters in to move a lot of it around. We're prepared to offer $300 for the partitioning, plus pay for the removal of the carpet, which we estimate will cost you $400 to lift. You will then to able to auction off the carpet for a price we estimate will be somewhere between $1000 and $1500."

The reply was less than enthusiastic. "All you've offered me is $300 cash," he grumbled. I repeated my offer stressing the total value of the package when the carpet was sold.

My line on the carpet was obviously causing a problem because he was becoming agitated. We seemed to be dead-locking when he blurted out, "I don't want the damned carpet!"

It seemed so irrational. After all, his firm owned it and we certainly weren't about to buy a carpet we wanted ripped out.

I bit my tongue to stop myself countering, "I'm sorry but the carpet is your problem" and instead probed with questions to discover what was behind his concern over the carpet. Piecing the answers together, it became clear my original proposal created a lot of extra work for him. He had just spent the last month moving out of our premises into new accommodation and the last thing he wanted was the hassle involved in getting carpet lifted and auctioned. It was also clear my original $300 cash was too low.

I therefore completely repackaged my proposal. "I tell you what," I proposed, "We'll offer you $1250 cash, we'll lift the carpet and we'll sell the carpet for you, provided we get 50% of the proceeds from the sale. This way you get extra cash, you don't have the worry of the carpet and we have an incentive to get a good price for the carpet." He readily agreed.

When we finally costed out the deal, the partitioning had cost us $850 ($1250 cash less the $400 we got as our share for the carpet). We had expected to pay between $3000 and $4500.

If the other party had done some homework and questioned us about our needs before detailing the proposal, the result could have been very different. Some quick homework on their part would have revealed that the replacement cost for the partitioning, which had been there four years, was $27,000. By allowing about $12,000 depreciation for wear and tear, their original figure of $15,000 could have been made to look credible.

Questions Make Us Think

Questions force us to do more than listen. Because they involve us, they stimulate us to use our thought processes constructively.

Questions encourage us to solve our own problems.

Imagine you're leading your section's budget meeting considering requests for additional capital expenditure. The production supervisor suggests replacing some existing machinery. You could easily squash the proposal declaring: "We can't afford the initial capital outlay. Our ongoing running and maintenance costs will rise. There's no demand for the extra output we'll produce."

In less than 30 seconds you could dispense with the idea. However you pause and turn your thoughts into questions.

- What will it initially cost?
- What do you estimate it will cost in ongoing servicing charges?
- What demand exists for the extra output?

If your initial analysis is right the supervisor will come to the same conclusion as you. Without putting him down you made him work through the problem.

There is also always a possibility your initial assumptions about the machinery were based on out of date or wrong information. When you make strong instantaneous assertions you are inviting others to join battle and prove you wrong. By turning your assertions into questions you get the credit, whatever the conclusions.

Questions Persuade

Good negotiators don't persuade by telling. They persuade by asking questions. They use questions to plant ideas in the other party's mind, and then get them to nurture them as if they were their own. Whereas questions move negotiators forward, statements often create roadblocks to be navigated around.

Most of us try to persuade others over to our point of view with reasons. Yet we are often highly resistant to being persuaded by reasons. Neil Rackham and the Huthwaite Research Group found in their negotiating research "that reasons will only work successfully in persuading people who are already on your side . . . If we're both in favour of a particular political policy, you'll be very receptive to any reasons I give for supporting it. But . . . if you're against the policy, the longer my list of reasons, the more you'll find counter arguments to support your existing opinion."[14]

Hence successful negotiators use questions, rather than reasons, as their main persuasive tools.

The accounting department in a large industrial conglomerate is split over the merits of a new computerised information system. The split has political implications, since the two camps developing reflect the staffing of the two old divisions that were recently merged.

Acting as a mediator, Craig Ellis, the Divisional Manager, calls a meeting and controls it through four key questions.

"What are the key features of each system?" he begins. "What features would an ideal system contain? What features do each of the proposed systems lack compared to the ideal system? How might we combine the best features of the two proposed systems?"

By the time the opinion leaders of the two camps had fully answered the last question, it was obvious a degree of consensus was emerging. They were beginning to treat the new ideas as their own.

Questions Diffuse Conflict

Since negotiation is a means of settling our differences, conflict in some form is always present. Questions help keep the lines of communication open. Skilled negotiators use questions as an alternative to open disagreement.

Instead of stating "your equipment will not stand up to the freezing temperatures we sometimes get here", ask "how will your equipment cope with the freezing temperature we sometimes get here?"

If the equipment won't cope, then it's much better that they admit, "Well, there could be some difficulties." If they try and bluff their way around the problem, you'll get a valuable insight into the character of the other person and the nature of the company you're considering doing business with. And if they do come up with an acceptable answer, then your objection would have been a waste of time and might have led to a putdown which could have soured a potentially useful relationship.

Questions Keep You in Control

Questions give you power to control the content, tone, pace and direction of a negotiation.

With questions you can control the issues you want to discuss – and also what you want to avoid. With questions you can set the mood and tone of a meeting. With questions you can slow down or force the pace of a discussion. With questions you can bring a negotiation back on track after losing direction.

Because the other party feels compelled to answer, the initiative invariably lies with the asker.

Questions Uncover Needs

The prime purpose of the exploration step is to uncover and develop needs. Look at how this skilled salesperson uses questions to probe for problems, difficulties and concerns, and gets the customer to state their needs.

Seller: What machines do you use for packaging?
Buyer: Four UAB 3200s.

Seller: Have your operators found any problems using them?
Buyer: Sometimes they find it difficult to change batches but we seem to be coping now.

Seller: Has this held up production at all?
Buyer: At first it did, but now we've trained four operators to use them.

Seller: Is there a problem when one goes sick or on holiday?
Buyer: We can live with that. However, the staff don't like using the UAB machines. They have to be continually monitored and adjusted, and staff keep leaving after a few months.

Seller: How does the extra turnover affect your training costs?
Buyer: Each extra worker we train costs us $2000 for UAB on-site training and $10,000 in wages and lost production. That's some $12,000 for each new

operator. So far we've had to train three new ones this year.

Seller: So that's $36,000 in extra training costs this year. Is there any drop off in quality while you're familiarising a new operator?

Buyer: Don't talk to me about that. I've spent much of the last two weeks soothing customers who are complaining about shoddy cartons. One batch of rejects was so large we had to subcontract out some of the work to keep faith with our largest customer.

Seller: From what you said, because the UAB machines are so difficult to use, you had to lay out $36,000 in training costs. Staff turnover is high, rejects are up. Your reject rate seems unacceptably high. Quality is suffering and you're getting irate customers.

Having used questions to uncover the buyer's needs the seller is now in an ideal position to sell his product by matching his product's features against the needs of the customer.

Questions Clarify Misunderstandings

Skilled negotiators constantly use questions to clarify views and positions. Cases are often presented ambiguously – sometimes deliberately. You therefore need to ask for more information or for more background. Clarification questions help build rapport.

Lead in with questions such as:

- Could you please explain that again.
- Could you please go over your concern about . . .
- Let me be sure, am I right in assuming you want . . .
- Am I right in thinking that . . .

- If I understand you correctly, are you saying you need . . .

Questions Test Assumptions

Skilful questioning allows you to test assumptions. For example, sales people often wrongly assume that price is the key issue, and as soon as the going gets tough they chop their price. Yet they can often test this assumption with a simple direct question.

A large sale of machine tools to a foreign customer has run into difficulties. You ask the customer, "What in our proposal concerns you?" They reply, "Your price is competitive but your warranty period is too short." You had assumed that your price was too high and that warranty was not an issue, especially given the number of industry quality awards you've won in the last few years.

Always check your assumptions before acting on them.

Open and Closed Questions

Questions can be loosely classified as *open* or *closed*. An open question is designed to generate a detailed response, whereas a closed question can be answered with a yes or no or with a brief statement of fact.

Start with Open Questions

Good negotiators start with open rather than closed questions. An open question requires an extended answer, so it cannot be answered with a simple "yes" or "no". Open ended questions are better than closed questions for drawing out information – they increase dialogue by drawing out and involving the other negotiator. So if a negotiation seems to be heading for deadlock it often pays to ask open questions.

Examples of open questions include:

- *What* problems are your having with . . .
- *How* do you calculate . . .
- *What* advantages could an improved . . .

After you've used open questions to fill in the background, you should narrow your focus and ask more specific or closed questions.

Use closed questions when you want to gather specific details or to shift the direction of the conversation. Use closed questions to pin the other side to a specific commitment.

Examples of closed questions include:

- Are you able to deliver by June 28?
- Can you change the specifications?
- Is a tolerance of 6mm sufficient?
- Do you prefer 3.5″ or 5″ disc drives?

We use closed questions far too much. Look at this example of an accounting software support salesperson using closed questions to extract information from a potential customer.

Seller: Does your company use Promax accounting software?

Customer: Yes.

Seller: Who is in charge of software management?

Customer: Our Financial Administrator.

Seller: Do you have an ongoing support contract?

Customer: Yes.

Seller: When does this support contract come up for renewal?

Customer: In October.

Seller: How do you rate the quality of your current
                 software support?
Customer: Reasonable.

By opening with a series of closed questions the seller has
turned the discussion into a cross-examination.

Imagine if the salesperson had started with open
questions.

Seller: Can you describe how your existing accounting
                 software support contract works?
Customer: Tomlin Software provide seven day a week
                 service for our Promax accounting software.
                 The base fee provides for 70 hours of phone
                 consultations, and any other work is charged
                 out at an agreed hourly rate.

Seller: How has Tomlin Software worked out?
Customer: Our staff found the phone support invaluable
                 while Alison Hollis was working there. Since
                 she left we've noticed we've had to get them
                 over here a lot more.

These two open questions have provided the seller with a
valuable lead on how he might approach the presentation
he wants to make when the software support contract comes
up for review.

Questions to Avoid
Good, constructive questions reduce tension, build effective working relationships and reveal needs.

Bad or destructive questions, however, generate
defensiveness, hostility and anger. Consider this classic
parent/child confrontation.

Parent: Where have you been?
Child: Out.

Parent: What did you do?
Child: Nothing.

The parent isn't really asking for information at all. The parent is accusing the child. The child knows that a truthful answer will result in trouble, so evades the issue – by answering, "Nothing."[15]

Avoid questions that:

- *Accuse.* Was it you coming back from lunch at 2:30 pm?

- *Reprimand.* Why didn't you complete this report on time?

- *Entrap.* Are you still beating your wife?

- *Force agreement.* This is the best deal – don't you agree?

- *Trick.* If sales increase next year, will you still propose cutting support services?

- *Threaten.* How do you expect more business, given your lousy service?

- *Pre-judge.* Why didn't you wait an extra week to receive ALCO's proposal? It could have saved us $250,000.

Indeed, avoid all questions where a question is a poor substitute for a more direct message.

The Art of Active Listening

"Knowing how to listen can double the effectiveness of your negotiating. Did you hear that?"

"We hear half of what is said, listen to half of what we hear, understand half of it, believe half of it and remember half of that," wrote one wit. If you listen this way, you are doomed as a negotiator.

What is Your Negotiation Ear Q?

To check how effective a listener you are, answer these ten questions.

1. Do you do most of the talking?

2. Do you get impatient and interrupt others?

3. Do you finish off the sentences of others?

4. Do you start arguing before the other person has finished their case?

5. Do you continually judge other people's messages as "believable" or "unbelievable"?

6. Do you switch off early and fake attention?

7. Do you listen for facts and not ideas?

8. Do you rarely give visual feedback? (Smile or nod in agreement.)

9. Do you get easily distracted by emotional language?

10. Do you allow yourself to be distracted by the person's appearance or personality?

If you answered yes to any of the questions then your Negotiation Ear Q needs raising.

Professional negotiators listen intently to the other side. They are active listeners and don't get distracted by emotion-laden words. They withhold judgement and try to understand the other person's point of view. They look behind the words spoken for the emotional content of the message transmitted by the subtleties of voice and body language. They appreciate that what is not said can be just as important as what is said.

Reflective Listening

One of the best ways to show you've heard and understood the other person is to *reflect* or *paraphrase* the content of what the other person has said.

Reflecting Content

Your desktop publishing supervisor is in your office, obviously annoyed.

"We can't keep up with all the demands on the new MacIntosh system," she says. "Nobody, particularly the departmental managers, is using the booking system. They all want everything yesterday. I don't know how I'm going to get your monthly performance report done."

You say: "It sounds like you're having trouble keeping some of the managers in line, is that what you're saying?"

That brief exchange shows the essentials of reflective listening.

An effective reflection is concise, simple and easily understood. If you get too wordy you can easily derail the speaker's train of thought.

An effective reflection gives the essence of the speaker's message and cuts right through the verbal clutter.

An effective reflection mirrors the speaker's own words. Above all, it demonstrates understanding. Don't fall into the trap of simply parroting the other person's words. Reflecting is not parroting. Parroting stunts conversations, whereas reflecting encourages discussion. So don't make the mistake of repeating the speaker's exact words.

Reflect content with phrases such as:

- It sounds like . . .
- In other words . . .
- So, . . .
- So, you're saying . . .
- It seems that . . .
- You mean . . .
- I guess . . .

Notice an effective reflection signals tentativeness. You don't know your interpretation is correct until the other person replies with "Yes, that's it!" or with some similar statement.

Reflecting Feelings

Effective listeners not only paraphrase facts, they reflect feelings as well. Anyone who speaks to you with an emotional overtone first wants their feelings understood and acknowledged.

Your office manager has begun a discussion with you about her career. She says: "I've been here four years, and I'm still doing the same old job. I could do it in my sleep. I had hoped I might have been able to do some of the accountant's work, but it's never eventuated."

You respond: "Seems like you're feeling bored and frustrated, is that it?"

By acknowledging the feelings, labelling them, and accepting them, you are laying the foundations for a productive discussion.

Reflective listening is an essential part of win-win negotiating. Good reflecting:

- Encourages the other person to keep talking.
- Corrects misunderstandings, false assumptions and misinterpretations.
- Reassures the speaker that you are listening.
- Gives you a much deeper insight into the needs of the other party.
- Helps you remember what was said.
- Builds rapport and mutual respect.

Summarising

Sometimes negotiations wander off course. To get the negotiation back on track summarise where you are at.

A summary refocuses attention on to the issues. Summaries should be short – no-one wants to hear a long drawn out account.

Summaries should be balanced and cover both sides' viewpoints and proposals. A one-sided summary will simply spark off more arguments, whereas a balanced summary can markedly improve the climate of the negotiation. If the other party thinks your summary is inaccurate, then ask them to do it until you both agree.

- I'm concerned, Peter, that we seem to have wandered off track. Let me see if I can summarise the main points we've covered.
- To prevent any misunderstanding I would just like to summarise the main points of our last meeting.
- Let me summarize the key issues as I see them.

Summarise during all phases of the negotiation, but especially:

- Whenever emotion and argument are clouding the issues.
- Whenever you feel your views are not being properly recognised, appreciated or understood.
- Whenever you feel it's time to conclude the agreement.
- After reaching agreement, to make sure your understanding of what has been agreed is exactly the same as theirs.

The Impact of Body Language

"Watch out for a man whose stomach doesn't move when he laughs."
Ancient Chinese Proverb

In the early 1900s, psychologist O. Pfungst became intrigued by the extraordinary ability of a remarkable horse called Hans. Hans seemingly possessed the skill to make rapid mathematical calculations.

After a problem was written on a blackboard placed before him, Hans quickly calculated the answer by tapping the low numbers with his right forefoot and multiples of 10 with his left.

Pfungst quickly rejected trickery as a possibility. Hans's owner had no financial motive. He did not make any money from the shows. More importantly, Hans could count accurately even when his owner was absent. Neither could Pfungst believe Hans possessed human-like brain power. There simply had to be a more logical explanation.

After many hours of horse watching, Pfungst cracked the mystery. Hans only ever performed in front of an audience that could see the blackboard and therefore knew the answer. As soon as the problem was written on the black-board, the audience leaned slightly forward to watch Hans' forefeet. Although the movement was slight, Hans picked it up and read it as a signal to start tapping. As the taps reached the right number, the audience tensed with excitement and unconsciously, with ever so slight head movements, signalled to Hans to stop tapping. The audience unwittingly provided the answer through their body language.

We all pick up body signals. Everyone of us constantly picks up and interprets these clues, even when we don't appreciate it.[16]

Whenever we speak, we use our faces, eyes, voice and body to reinforce our words.

The unspoken messages we pick up account for most of the impact of any message we receive. In forming an impression we first focus on what we can see. Albert Mehrabian, one of the foremost authorities on non verbal communication claims 55 percent of the meaning of a message is transmitted by just facial expressions and body language.[17]

Second, we pick up the speaker's voice – their rate of speech, volume, pitch and tone. Voice (excluding the actual words) can convey up to 38 percent of the meaning in a face-to-face meeting.

Finally we listen to the actual words – which add just seven percent to the meaning.

"It's not that your words are unimportant," says communication expert Janet Elsea. "But if others do not like what they see, or if they get past your body language only to be stopped by something in your voice, they may not care at all about what you say. Their minds may be made up, their first impressions indelibly formed."[18] Effective communicators therefore synchronise their body, voice and words – so what is said is reinforced by how it is said.

When verbal and non-verbal messages contradict each other, we believe the body language and tone of voice before the actual words.[19]

Your manager is reading your board report on rationalisation, while you wait expectantly. After she has finished flicking through it, you ask "What do you think?" She shrugs her shoulders, frowns, swivels her chair away from you and mumbles, "It's okay, I guess. It's fine." Do you believe her? Probably not. Her dejected body language is a better indication of her true feelings. You should press further to find out what is concerning her.

How to Read the Other Person

Gestures. To correctly interpret body language you must observe gestures in clusters. One of the worst mistakes you can make is to make an interpretation on the basis of a single gesture. A scratch of the head can signal, among other things, doubt, apprehensiveness, deceit, forgetfulness, or headlice. Crossed legs cause similar problems. Crossed legs generally signal a defensive attitude. However, problems arise when interpreting female body language. Many women have been trained as children to sit "like a lady" with legs or ankles crossed.

Non-verbal cues usually occur in congruent clusters – groups of gestures and movements that are consistent with each other and reinforce the meaning of the words that go with them.

Context. All gestures should be considered in the context in which they occur. If, for example, your boss is sitting with his arms and legs tightly crossed and chin down and the heating system has broken down, it very likely means he's cold, not defensive.

While many of the body gestures are the same all over the world, non-verbal signals such as eye contact can differ enormously from culture to culture. Most western cultures train their young to "look a person in the eyes", whereas most Japanese and Polynesians find sustained eye contact embarrassing. Tradition teaches that it is disrespectful to look someone – especially a senior – directly in the eye.

To create a positive, open, non-verbal climate that is conducive to a win-win negotiation:

- Face your opposite number squarely
- Assume an open posture
- Lean forward
- Maintain eye contact
- Relax[20]

1. **Face your opposite number squarely**. Most people focus on your face as their first cue to gauge your attitude, feelings and emotional state.

   Show interest by looking directly at the other person. Tilt your head slightly to one side, arch your eyebrows and nod intermittently to show you understand or agree. Also cultivate a relaxed yet enthusiastic smile.

   For a cluster of negative gestures, watch a hostile negotiator who "typically looks at you with eyes wide open, and corners of his eyebrows down and sometimes even talks through his teeth with very little movement of lips."[21]

2. **Assume an open posture**. When you sit with legs un-crossed and slightly apart, you convey warmth and openness. Open hands also signal you're sincere and open to new ideas.

   Leading negotiating authorities, Gerard Nierenberg and Henry Calero, found in their research that whenever negotiations went well, seated participants unbuttoned their coats, uncrossed their legs, sat forward in their chairs and moved closer to the other side. This "getting together cluster" was usually accompanied by words which stressed common needs and the positive advantages of agreement.[22]

On the other hand, if you cross your arms and legs, you are adopting a negative or defensive posture. Locked ankles and clenched fists also communicate defensiveness.

Nierenberg and Calero found the locking of ankles by one party often signals the holding back of a valuable concession. With skilled questioning you can unlock the ankles and uncover the concession.

3. **Lean forward**. When you lean forward in a chair with your hands on your knees towards the other party, you are indicating interest. You are also showing you are listening and are ready to proceed.

   If, however, you sit back in your chair with your hands "sharply steepled" you are indicating indifference. A barrier such as a desk between you and the other party can also add to the negative feelings.

4. **Maintain Eye Contact**. If you want to communicate interest and empathy, look the other person in the eye. When we like someone, or find them interesting or appealing, we look at them a lot – research shows about 60 to 70 percent of the time. Our eye pupils dilate at the same time. Hostility is also associated with sustained eye contact but the pupils constrict, so the look feels like a stare.

   When we are nervous, we avoid eye contact – our eyes typically meet the other person's less than 40 per cent of the time. As a result, other people feel uneasy or distrust us.

5. **Relax**. A comfortable, relaxed, yet attentive pose lets the other person know that you're ready to listen. A relaxed posture signals openness while a tense, rigid posture indicates defensiveness.

   Don't slouch or appear bored. And do try to avoid fidgeting and other random movements which communicate impatience, boredom and nervousness.

Practise your observation skills at airports, parties, or wherever people meet. Alternatively, video a favourite television programme. Turn the sound off and, using a photocopy of the checklist of gestures contained in Appendix One as a guide, tick off the gestures you observe. Then turn the sound up to check the accuracy of your readings. Sustained practice of this sort will quickly sharpen your body language reading skills.

During a negotiation it pays to take periodic mental snapshots of yourself and ask, "What signals am I sending with my face, arms, legs and body at this moment?"

When reading body language always observe clusters of gestures within the context in which they occur. Never make interpretations on the basis of a single gesture.

The Power of Vocal Control

"In 1985, Peter Blanck and his associate researchers proved that California juries were twice as likely to convict defendants in criminal trials when judges knew of prior felony convictions, even though the law forbids judges to share that information with juries – and that the factor responsible for the difference was nothing more than the judges' *tone of voice*."[23]

81

After body language, your voice has the biggest impact on the meaning of any message you send. As much as 38% of the meaning of a message is communicated by the quality of your voice.

If you sound energetic and confident, very likely you will be viewed as energetic and confident. If you sound weak and timid, you will probably be seen as weak and timid. If you sound shrill and strident, people will probably treat you that way. Your voice can reveal how relaxed or tense you are, how tired you are and even indicate your emotional state, so it's important you know what you sound like.

The only effective way you can really test how your voice is heard by others is to listen to a tape recording. As you listen to your voice on tape, ask yourself: Does my voice reflect the words I am speaking? Is there anything about my voice that I dislike? Normally you'll be your harshest critic, so do check with others.

If your voice needs improvement, practise with a tape recorder by speaking or reading onto it. Keep varying your voice until you create the right sound. A number of books such as *First Impression, Best Impression* by Janet Elsea contain useful exercises.[24] If it is still causing concern, then consult a professional such as a speech therapist or a voice coach, or join a community group which specialises in speech training.

A clear, confident, pleasant voice is a valuable asset for any negotiator – especially one who wants to build a positive climate. In any case, it is essential your voice is congruent with your body language and the words you speak.

Using Assertive Language

If your body language and voice are in congruence, the other party will listen to the words you speak.

Effective negotiators use assertive rather than aggressive or passive language to state clearly what they want, feel and think. Aggressive speakers' words put people down. When attacked by aggressive speakers, we often take their words personally and counter in kind.

Passive speakers, on the other hand, communicate submissiveness and docility through their words and thereby weaken any position they are trying to present.

In contrast, assertive speakers choose words which convey strength and authority. Assertive speakers put themselves forward without ever putting the other person down. They speak clearly, directly and use lots of "I's".

Your plant supervisor is a poor manager of time. The staff often wait around for their daily jobs to be allocated, and they are falling behind schedule. You call him in and say:

Aggressive *or* Passive	**Assertive**
What's the matter, can't you organise yourself? You're not managing very well.	I want you to schedule your time so the production staff are all assigned their daily jobs by 9.00 a.m.
or	*or*
We were hoping you'd be able to push the workers along a little faster. Is that possible?	I need a guarantee that all the daily work for the shift is assigned by 9.00 am. I want you to make this top priority each morning.

Be Direct. Focus on your needs. When you assert your needs, focus sharply on what you want. Be specific. Ask yourself, "What precisely do I need?"

Make Assumptions Explicit. Don't expect others to read your mind. Don't assume others will know what needs like "better organised" or "better quality" mean.

Wait. Once you've clearly and briefly stated your needs, pause and wait for a reaction. Check to see that your needs have been understood. If they haven't, paraphrase your original statement.

Don't Weaken the Impact. Don't undermine your position and damage your credibility with weak powerless language. Statements such as:

- You may not agree with me *but* . . .
- This may not be what you're thinking, *however* . . .
- I'm not 100% certain *but* . . .

convey ambivalence and apprehension and, when accompanied by non-assertive body language, lessen the impact of your statements.

Successful win-win negotiating requires a dual focus. You need to be able to focus on both your and the other side's needs. Too much concern for the other side's needs, however, can work against you. Active listening, when combined with assertiveness, helps you maintain the right balance – and results in problem solving which seeks to satisfy both parties.

Using Silence for Effect

"Silence is one of the hardest things to refute."
Josh Billings

Many people associate silence with anxiety, hostility, awkwardness or shyness. Yet silence can be a powerful communication tool if used effectively.

The noise of a silence can sometimes be deafening. If you feel uncomfortable with silence, and many of us do, simply focus on the other person's body language. Some people need to think through their ideas without talking, but don't expect much eye contact at this stage. It's very difficult to maintain eye contact when you're deep in thought. The silences which sometimes seem like hours are rarely more than 60 seconds.

Stop talking and stay silent until the other side speaks immediately after you have:

- Presented a proposal.
- Summarised progress.
- Asked a question.

Seasoned negotiators use silence to induce opponents to reveal more information than they intend to.

You are negotiating with the only local supplier of an important component. The supplier's salesperson says, "These components will never be cheaper than they are now."

You stay silent.

The salesperson adds, "You will be looking to buy more of this line in June and July, won't you?"

You stay silent.

The salesperson continues, "Look, we begin the Sensui contract on 1st May. It's a huge deal and our production lines will be committed for the next couple of years. Prices for small orders the size you typically order will rise over 20%."

As negotiators, we should all remind ourselves that we have two ears, two eyes, and one mouth and they should be used in that proportion. In other words, don't talk to fill the silence.

Reading Between the Lines

"Words are empty cups: what you put in is not nearly so important as knowing what the other person is likely to take out."

James J. Cribbin

Many statements we make or hear have double meanings. The first meaning is the basic information contained in the actual words. The second, the hidden meaning, is the real message. In other words, we say one thing and mean another. When we use *meta-talk* – as it is called – we say one thing and mean another.

Meta-talk is part and parcel of every negotiation. Sometimes it's amusing just listening to the meta-talk and working out the real meanings.

Most experienced negotiators have heard these:

- Our position is very firm and we are deeply committed to our goals and objectives.
  Implication: Don't expect us to make concessions without a real struggle.

- In consideration of our long association and mutual interests, we want to present this proposal, which we think is most fair and reasonable.
  Implication: We know you well enough to think you probably won't fall for this one, but we're going to test it on you anyway.

- Although I have been given full authority to settle . . .
  Implication: I will have to clear any further concessions with my organisation.

Certain words and phrases crop up time and time again in meta-messages. Whenever someone wants to downplay the importance of what they want to say they use *incidentally*.

"I really appreciated the great work you did on the landscaping. *Incidentally*, is it okay to pay your account monthly instead of weekly?"

"By the way", "before I forget", "while I think of it", serve the same purpose.

Whenever you hear "only" or "just" your ears should perk up and consider why the person is trying to downplay the importance of what is being said.

- It *only* represents one percent of the cost.
  Implication: As a percentage the figure is small but the actual cost is enormous.

- I was *just* being frank.
  Implication: Can't you take the truth.

While meta-words such as *incidentally* are stale and unimaginative, others such as *frankly, honestly* and *sincerely* often backfire on the user.

- *Frankly*, this is as far as I can go.
- *Honestly*, this is the best offer I can make.
- *Sincerely*, this is the best deal we've ever had.

When many people hear these meta-words they intuitively think the speaker is trying to deceive them. Unfortunately, many honest people preface their statements with these sorts of words, so beware!

Words such as fair, reasonable, and generous also irritate and offend.

- I'm a fair person.
  Implication: You are unfair.

- This is a generous offer.
  Implication: You're greedy if you don't accept it.

Always avoid irritators such as these. They invariably sour the climate. Neil Rackham's and John Carlisle's[25] research showed top negotiators are very careful to avoid them.

People also resent having meta-language used to manipulate or entrap them.

- Peter is *obviously* the best person for the job, *don't you agree?*

The phrasing here is designed to push the listener into a corner.

"As you are aware", "no doubt", "don't you feel" can similarly be used as manipulators.

Negotiators who use a lot of meta-talk, don't realise how transparent they are. Tune into your own use of meta-talk. Listen to the way you speak when you're trying to avoid being direct. This will alert you to what you have to listen for in others.

When you suspect someone is using meta-talk check it out by repeating the words over in your mind, listening to the way each word has been emphasised.

If it doesn't bother you, simply file away your interpretation for later use. If meta-talk is fouling the negotiation, raise it diplomatically with the other party.

Step Two: Exploring Each Other's Needs

Checkpoints:

- Communicate your opening position.

- Discover your opponent's position.

- Ask lots of questions.

- Start with open questions.

- Finish with closed questions.

- Avoid destructive questions.

- Reflect the content of the other side.

- Reflect the other side's feelings.

- Summarise where you are at.

- Create a positive, open non-verbal climate.

- Speak clearly and confidently.

- Use assertive language.

- Use silence for effect.

- Translate the meta-talk.

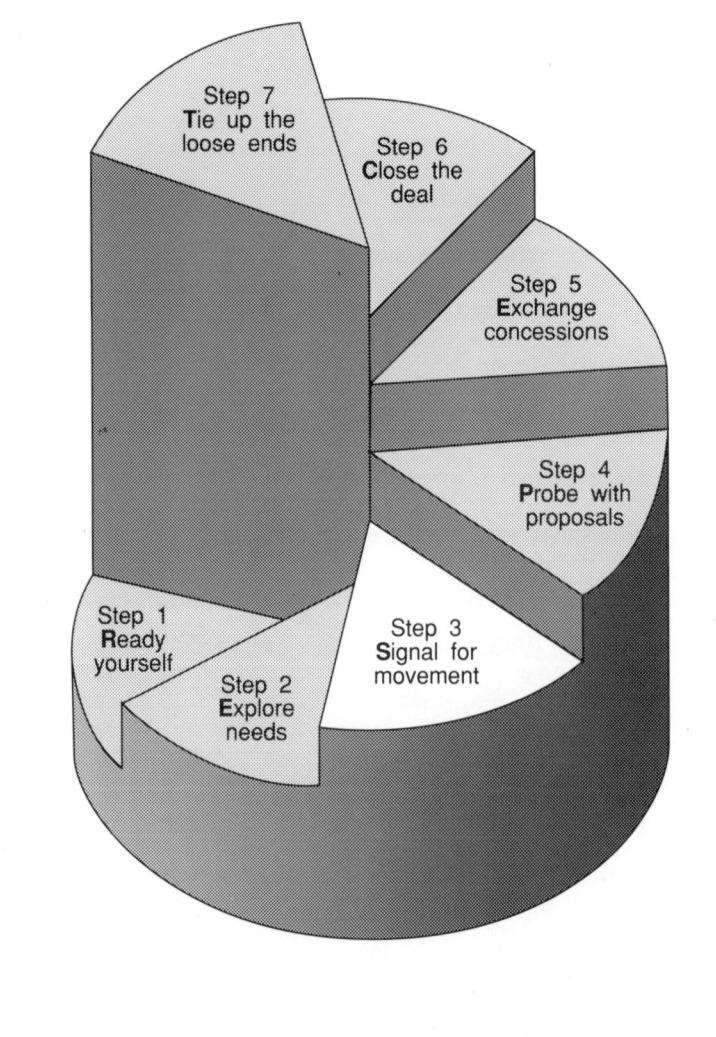

R-E-S-P-E-C-T
The seven steps to agreement

Step 7
Tie up the
loose ends

Step 6
Close the
deal

Step 5
Exchange
concessions

Step 4
Probe with
proposals

Step 1
Ready
yourself

Step 2
Explore
needs

Step 3
Signal for
movement

CHAPTER SIX

Step Three: Signalling for Movement

*"The journey of 1000 miles
starts with a single step"*

Chinese proverb

Negotiations often start out with both sides taking strong, seemingly-immovable opening positions. The opening statements are strong, unconditional and unqualified. For example:

- We do not give discounts.
- There is no chance of us moving on that point.
- That is not possible.

What is a Signal

A successful negotiation, however, depends on movement, and to reach agreement parties must move toward each other. Therefore, after a period of discussion or argument, one side will often subtly change their language to show that they are willing to move. These messages, indicating a willingness to move, are called *signals*.

For example, one party initially declares: "It is *impossible* to change our delivery schedule." After some discussion it changes to: "We would find it *extremely difficult* to meet that schedule."

The original, absolute statement has been *qualified*.

Signals allow negotiators to move from their opening position without giving an impression to the other negotiator that they are about to cave in.

How to Signal

Most people miss signals because they are not listening properly. The result can be prolonged argument. Because signals are, by definition, subtle changes in the language, they're easily missed. Often they are dropped into the middle of long rambling sentences. Negotiators who get caught up in point scoring and attacking the opponent's position therefore often miss signals.

To signal your willingness to move, simply add qualifications to your statements. For example:

- We do not *normally* give credit.
- We cannot meet *all* of your requests.
- Your timetable is *too* inflexible.

These qualified statements should generate replies such as:

- Under what circumstances do you give credit?
- Which request can you not meet?
- What changes do you require in the timetable?

From an argument, you have moved towards a concrete proposal.

Questioning for Clarification

Don't ever punish the signaller with discussion killers, such as: "I see you've finally decided to modify your ridiculous opening offer", or "It's about time you decided to move."

Instead, reinforce signalling behaviour by asking questions that encourage the other person to elaborate. For example: "Could you possibly clarify under what circumstances you would be willing to change your production schedule?"

A signal is not simply a message that shows the other side is prepared to move, it is also a call for you to move. The signaller is in effect saying, "If you show you're willing to move from your opening position, then we're willing to negotiate further."

The best way to reinforce signalling behaviour is therefore to reciprocate with a signal that you're also prepared to move. If the other party misses your signal, repeat it or reword it. It may have been misunderstood.

Step Three: Signalling for Movement

Checkpoints:

- Listen intently for signals showing movement.

- Clarify all signals with follow up questions.

- Reciprocate with your own signals.

- Repeat or reword missed signals.

R-E-S-P-E-C-T
The seven steps to agreement

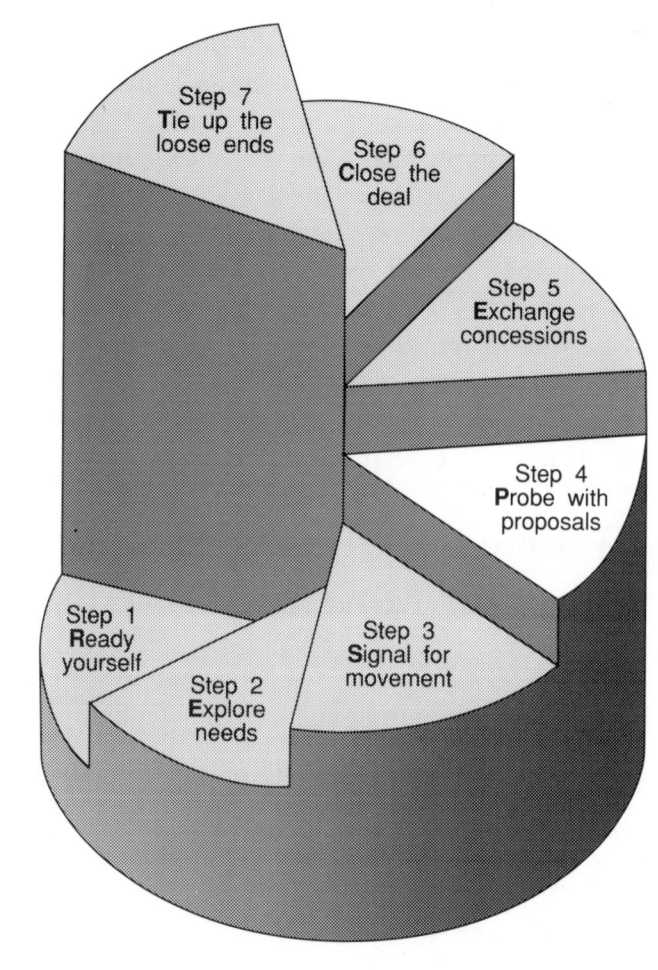

CHAPTER SEVEN

Step Four:
Probing with Proposals

*"Successful collaborative negotiation
lies in finding out what the other side
really wants and showing them a way to get it,
while you get what you want."*

Herb Cohen

Once a positive signal has been received, negotiations move to the proposal phase. Here both sides probe each other for areas of further movement by putting up proposals, or tentative offers, to address their needs and concerns.

What is a Proposal?

A proposal is a tentative suggestion for resolving differences. A union negotiator might propose, "If you will increase the base rate by eight percent, then I'll consider recommending to my members a reduction in manning levels."

Here the union official is being deliberately tentative because he is using the proposal as a means of eliciting information and generating movement.

By contrast, a "bargain" is a specific offer to resolve an issue. Here is the same union official making a *specific* offer. "If you increase the hourly rate by eight percent then we will recommend cutting manning levels in the boiler room by two staff."

Whereas the proposal is designed to *elicit information*, the bargaining phase focuses on trading concessions.

Presenting Proposals

Proposals should be kept conditional. State your condition first and be specific.

Use the if/then technique

- *If* you will cut your price by $6000 *then* we will consider increasing the size of our order.
- *If* you will increase sick leave to seven days *then* we will look at our claim for medical insurance.

In these examples the condition comes first. If you do X (a specific action) then I'll look at Y (a vague promise).

When you present a proposal, you can't avoid giving away information about your *settlement range*. This is why your proposal is explicit about what you want the other side to do and vague about what you're prepared to do.

Phrases such as "I'll consider", "I'll see what I can do", "I'll look at it" are typical offers included in proposals.

By clarifying the priorities of both sides, proposals and counter proposals move negotiators one step closer to agreement. Out of the cut and thrust of proposals and counter proposals, solutions to seemingly insolvable problems often emerge.

Keep your proposals brief. Then, go quiet until your opponent replies. Long explanations can reveal too much about your priorities.

Receiving Proposals

Proposals are matched by counter-proposals.

Never interrupt a proposal. Interruptions antagonise the speaker and a concession may be tagged on at the end.

Don't instantly reject a proposal. Above all, avoid the proposal killer "I disagree". Listen carefully, and treat it with respect.

Try not to say no. A "no" strangles discussion and halts movement.

Don't immediately counter with your own proposal. The worst time to present a counter proposal is just after the other side has put their proposal. People are in their least receptive frame of mind to opposing ideas when they have just presented their own. Skilled negotiators instead use this time to ask lots of questions such as:

- How would your proposal work given our special requirements?
- Wouldn't that proposal create difficulties for our head office staff?
- How would your proposal get over the security problem?

Give as detailed a response as possible. A detailed response provides opportunities for further signals.

Indicate areas of agreement. If the negotiation has involved a number of proposals, point out places where agreement might be possible.

Regularly summarise where you are at. Not only do summaries remind people, they show that you are actively listening and keep the negotiations on track.

Packaging

Proposing allows both sides to plot out the key variables in the negotiation and determine each other's priorities.

In a typical negotiation lots of proposals end up on the table. Some are incompatible, but others overlap or complement each other. By juggling and reshuffling proposals you can often repackage the parcel of proposals into a mutually acceptable package.

Multiply the Variables

Effective negotiators try to multiply the number of variables, as each new variable creates more options for packaging. The more variables, the less likelihood there is of deadlock. The more variables, the better the chance of a win-win agreement.

Negotiations had reached an impasse over the sale of Gary McGeehan's house. Gary wanted $230,000, the prospective buyer was only prepared to go to $210,000. Neither side seemed prepared to budge.

In desperation Gary turned to his neighbour, Alyson Doyle, a professional mediator, for advice.

"Gary, you seem to be deadlocked on a single issue – price," said Alyson. "You're locked in a classic single issue win-lose confrontation. Whoever concedes loses at the other's expense.

"Whenever you're headed for deadlock in what appears to be a single issue negotiation, try multiplying the number of variables. Think, for example, of some of the possible variables that are negotiable when you buy and sell a house.

Does the price include the fittings, carpets, furniture and fixtures? These can always be isolated out as negotiable items.

"If you were buying a house, for example, you could try and add in conditions which require the seller to correct any defects in the property. In the house we're in now, I included a condition requiring the seller to complete the back garden block wall. Completing the wall would have involved me in a lot of hassle and expense. The owner happened to be a builder so it was relatively inexpensive and easy for him to fix it up.

"The preferred occupation date is another variable. They may want to delay settlement date because they want time to sell their other house.

"Why don't you draw up a list of all the possible variables you can think of. When you identify lots of issues, it becomes possible to link concessions in one area with concessions in another. You then trade concessions by giving the other party some of what they really want in exchange for receiving what is really valuable to you. That's essentially what negotiating is all about. If you get stuck, call me at home over the weekend."

Gary did call. "We've settled," Gary enthused. "It seems so simple now. I agreed to cut my price to $220,000 and the buyer has agreed to delay occupation date for three months. That means we won't have to rent another house while we wait for our new house to be completed. I've also agreed to finish lining the garage with plasterboard."

Step Four:
Probing with Proposals

Checkpoints:

- Probe to elicit information.

- Use proposals to clarify priorities.

- Propose, then go quiet.

- State your condition first and be specific.

- Use the if/then technique.

- Never interrupt a proposal.

- Don't instantly reject a proposal.

- Avoid the proposal killer "I disagree".

- Don't immediately counter with your own proposal.

- Give as detailed a response as possible.

- Indicate areas of agreement.

- Regularly summarise where you are at.

- Repackage proposals to make them more acceptable.

- Multiply the variables to create more options and win-win packages.

R-E-S-P-E-C-T
The seven steps to agreement

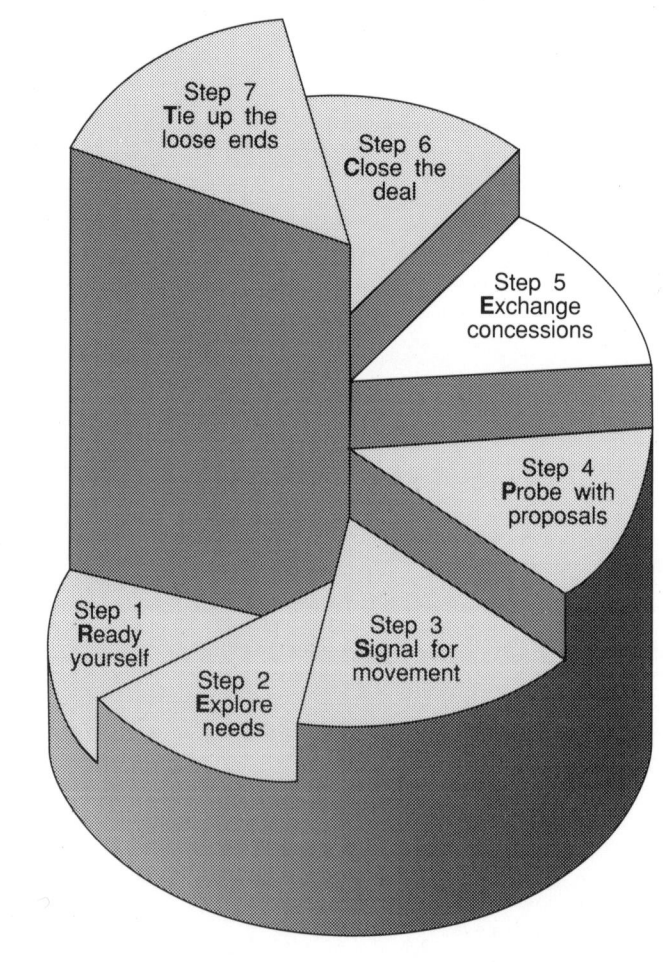

CHAPTER EIGHT

Step Five:
Exchanging Concessions

An actor, negotiating a contract
with movie mogul Sam Goldwyn, demanded
"fifteen hundred a week."

"You're not asking fifteen hundred
a week," snapped back Goldwyn, "you're
asking twelve hundred and I'm
giving you a thousand."

So far we've gone through the steps of preparing, communicating our opening positions and exploring both sides' needs. We've signalled our willingness to move and probed with proposals to find areas of possible agreement. Now we're ready to get down to trading – or exchanging concessions.

Calculate the value of every concession. Before even making a concession ask yourself:

- What value is the concession to the other party?
- What will it cost me?
- What do I need in return?

This is critically important. Don't forget the *could get, should get, must get* framework you used while preparing to determine your objectives. The basis of successful bargaining is to trade your *could gets* so you can get your *must gets*.

How to Make Concessions

Link issues. Before you start trading concessions, get all of the other party's demands on the table. Then make it clear that any concession on any one item is conditional upon agreement on the other outstanding issues.

Don't fall into the trap of negotiating piecemeal, that is, dealing with one issue at a time. It often seems common sense to deal with issues one at a time, but negotiators who do can end up being chopped up like a piece of salami. Typically, you make concessions in the early stages then find you don't have enough concessions left to trade for the more extreme demands which come later. Treat all issues as part of a single package. So link a concession on issue A to a small concession on issue B and possibly major concessions on issues C and D.

Create room to move. Whenever you make an offer, give yourself plenty of room to negotiate. If you're selling, start high. If you're buying, start low. Opening positions, however, should always be realistic and credible. If you can't justify your demand, don't make it. Ridiculous demands simply generate hostility.

Avoid making the first major concession. If you can, get the other party to make the first concession, especially on a major issue. Chester L. Karrass found, in his experiments, that losers generally made the first concessions on major issues. So if you do have to make the first concession to get momentum going, make it on a minor issue.

Control your concession rate. Winning negotiators control their concession rate much better than losers. Successful negotiators make smaller concessions, are less generous and less predictable. And they don't crack under deadline pressure.

Karrass found losers have less control. While many give away little in the first half of a negotiation, most cave in later with a series of large concessions.

Different concession rates send different messages. Examine these four concession patterns of sellers cutting their prices over four separate negotiation sessions.

Differing Concession Rates

Negotiation	1	2	3	4
Concession 1	0	200	95	395
Concession 2	0	200	190	265
Concession 3	0	200	250	120
Concession 4	800	200	265	20
Total Conceded	800	800	800	800

Negotiation 1's pattern (0-0-0-800) reveals the seller has held firm until the end and then made a major concession. This concession pattern will encourage strong buyers to hold out for more.

Negotiation 2's pattern (200-200-200-200) is remarkable for its consistency, but will achieve little except to encourage the buyer to hold out for a further concession.

Negotiation 3's pattern (95-190-250-265) would normally be disastrous. It simply encourages the buyer to raise their expectations.

Negotiation 4's pattern (395-265-120-20) indicates a willingness to negotiate but clearly signals the seller has reached their limit.

Karrass concludes from his experiments on concession rates that "the ideal way to handle negotiations if you are a buyer is to start low and give in slowly over a longer period of time. If you are a seller, just turn it around. Start high and give in slowly over a long period of time."[27]

Trade reluctantly. Make the other side toil for every concession they get. People appreciate concessions they have to work hard for. Don't devalue your concessions with remarks such as "I'll throw in free delivery" or "I'll knock off $1500." Comments such as these simply encourage the other side to ask for more.

Make small concessions. Don't give large concessions. Instead, give a series of small ones. In Karrass's experiments successful bargainers made consistently smaller concessions than their opponents.

Small concessions signal firmness. If you give away a large concession, you are acknowledging your previous position wasn't credible. Large concessions often raise the expectations of the other side.

Be patient – concede slowly. Negotiators who move too fast easily lose control. Quick negotiations are characterised by rapid concession making which are invariably disastrous for one side or the other.

Conserve your concessions. Don't give away your concessions too early. Be prepared to make the other party wait. They appreciate them more. Since you often need a concession or two to close a deal, you should always hold some concessions in reserve.

Demand reciprocation. Never give away a concession without getting a concession in return. Don't give away anything for nothing. Everything should be conceded in exchange for something else.

Make all concessions conditional. To protect yourself from giving away free concessions, preface all your offers with a condition. Use the if/then formula.

- *If* you agree to A, *then* I will agree to B.
- *If* you will increase your discount to 42.5%, *then* I will pay within seven days.

Justify all concessions. Don't give away concessions without supporting justification. "We've been looking at our component's costings, and we can lower our price by $4350 now that we've been able to source it from a new Korean based supplier."

Calculate the relative concession rates. By calculating the relative speeds of your and the other party's concessions you can get a good idea of how you are progressing.

Let's imagine you're involved in negotiation where both sides have made four price concessions. Your concessions total $60,000, theirs total $48,000. You're conceding $5 for every $4 they concede. The relative concession rate is, therefore, 5:4.

It's always useful to calculate the concession rate you will need to reach an acceptable settlement.

Let's say you have offered $200,000 to purchase a warehouse and you are prepared to go to $220,000. They have offered to sell it for $250,000. To reach an acceptable price they will have to concede $30,000, you can only concede $20,000. They have to concede three dollars for every two dollars you concede: a relative concession rate of 3:2.

Avoid tit-for-tat concessions. Don't fall into the trap of matching the other side's concessions. If they concede $800 worth of concessions try offering $600. If they protest, reply, "I'm sorry, but that's all we can afford."

Likewise, don't give a concession simply because it's your turn. If they're prepared to keep conceding without a reciprocal concession from you, let them. They may have more room to concede than you have.

Be wary of split the difference offers. I know a buyer who commonly makes a low opening offer, raises it a little, then offers to "split the difference". It's remarkable how often the other party falls for it. On the surface it seems so reasonable, but when you analyze the split it always seems to favour the proposer.

Before you agree to any such offer, calculate where the split will occur and where this fits into your settlement range. If you turn such an offer down, grab the initiative back by countering with your own proposal. Say: "I'm sorry I can't afford to split the difference but this is what I can do."

Track all concessions. As you keep track of all the offers and concessions, patterns should emerge which give insights into your opponent's priorities. If, for example, a buyer has conceded twice on price, agreed to pay for after hours service, but refuses to budge on the advance payment, the advance payment is the top priority. You can then question the reasons for this priority. Perhaps they have cash flow problems.

Similarly, if you want others to understand your priorities, send signals that reinforce those priorities. If quality is of paramount importance, make sure your words, body language and offers conform to that priority.

How to Build Momentum

Emphasise common interests. To keep the momentum rolling during the concession trading, continually emphasise the common interests of both sides, regularly summarise the progress you've made so far and constantly state your willingness to trade.

Reward concessions. When the other side grants a concession, reward it, don't punish it. Say: "I appreciate that", rather than "That's not good enough" or "Is that all?" Avoid making statements such as "This is my final offer" or "this is as far as I can go" too early. These effectively say to the other side "take it or leave it" when you really should be communicating, "We're closing the gap between us so let's keep moving forward."

Don't turn minor issues into matters of principle. Once you've forced the other side to make a stand where backing down involves a loss of face, you've created major difficulties. So if the other side makes a ridiculous stand, don't rub it in. Leave them an escape route which allows them to gracefully back down. Similarly, plan escape routes which will allow you to back down without losing face. For example, "Our designers have come up with a different component combination which will allow us to cut our price without any loss of performance."

Shift issues at impasses. If you are getting bogged down and seem to be deadlocking, shift issues. Don't insist on settling a particular issue before moving on to another subject.

Handle the ridiculous offer with care. Don't simply quit a negotiation when the other party makes a ridiculous offer. Rather than storm out, stay cool and polite. Say: "I'd like to do business with you but we're obviously miles apart at the moment. Perhaps you'd like to reconsider your offer and call me back when you've had a chance to re- examine your data."

Step Five:
Exchanging Concessions

Checkpoints:

- Link issues, don't trade piecemeal.

- Give yourself plenty of room to negotiate.

- If you're selling, start high.

- If you're buying, start low.

- All offers should be realistic and credible.

- Control and monitor your concession rate.

- Avoid making the first major concession.

- Trade reluctantly.

- Make small concessions.

- Make sure the other side reciprocates.

- Concede slowly.

- Conserve concessions for last minute trades.

- Preface all offers with a condition.

- Justify all concessions.

- Track all concessions – yours and theirs.

- Build momentum by emphasising common interests.

- Reward, don't punish, concessions.

- Don't turn minor issues into matters of principle.

- Shift issues at impasses.

- Handle ridiculous offers with care.

R-E-S-P-E-C-T

The seven steps to agreement

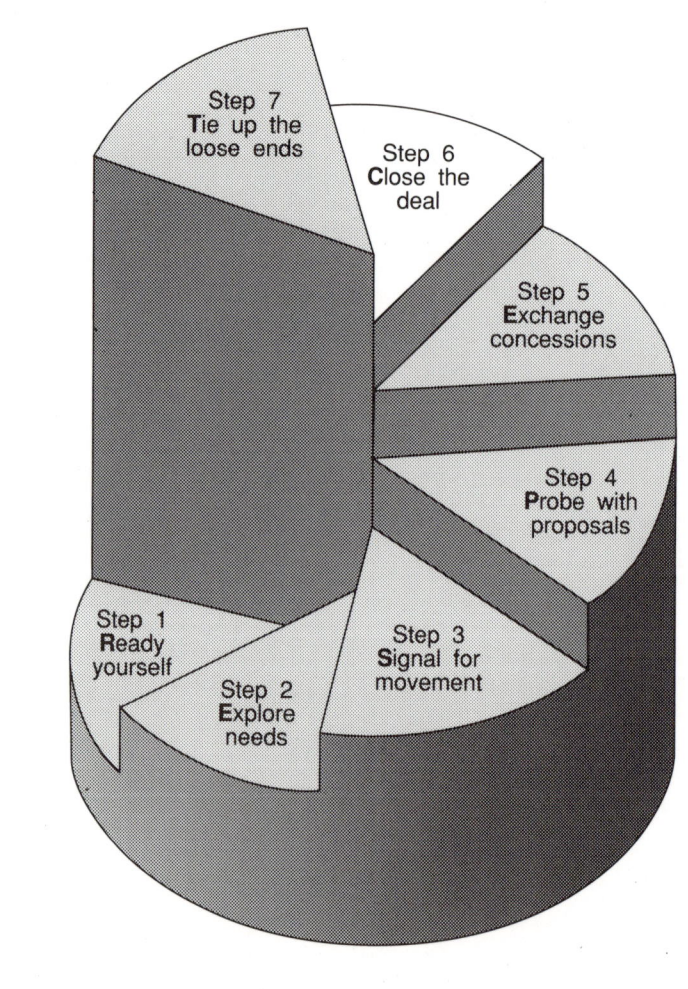

CHAPTER NINE

Step Six: Closing the Deal

"I always win. You always lose. What could be fairer than that."

Ashleigh Brilliant

You've been making concessions. So has the other side. But now you're getting close to your limit. How do you bring the negotiation to an end?

Timing the Close

Judging when to close is always difficult. Start by looking for signals in the body language of the other party.

- The chief executive of a foodstore chain, sitting arms crossed with locked ankles, uncrosses his legs and leans forward in the chair and moves closer to the senior partner of a legal firm who is presenting a proposal to take over the company's legal services.

- The manager, who was slouching and appearing bored during the debate over research and development expenditure, suddenly sits up and appears interested.

- The buyer, who appeared indifferent and was fidgeting as the salesperson talked, stops and listens attentively.
- The owner of a private company starts focusing on the finer technical points of a management buyout proposal.
- The purchasing officer for a large industrial hire firm repeatedly tests the demonstration front end loader.
- The project engineer keeps going back to the sample componentry and picks it up looking for possible defects.

All of these can be signals that the other party is close to agreement or has made up their mind.

You should also listen closely to the other party's words for indications they are ready to close. Listen out for questions such as:

- Can you have your auditors in here by April 6?
- When can I get delivery?
- When do we have to pay for it?
- How could we extend the warranty from 18 months to two years?
- What is the minimum order required for the binding machines?
- When could you begin training our staff?

These often mean the other side has already mentally agreed and is ready to close.

The Trial Close

Weak or inexperienced negotiators, unsure of when to close, keep conceding until the other side, overwhelmed by generosity, agrees. To overcome the problem of closing too late, sales staff have developed the *trial close*. As the name implies the trial close is a test to see how near the prospect is to buying.

Sellers test the waters with questions such as:

- Where would you install our machine?
- If you were to acquire this, would you prefer the economy or deluxe model?
- If you were to go ahead with this, would you feel better with the premium 24 hour seven day service contract or the standard working hours level of support?

Used effectively, trial closes will give you valuable information on how near the other side is to making a commitment.

Unfortunately, once sales staff overcome the fear of closing and of closing too late, many go to the opposite extreme by closing too often and too early.

Consider this example:

Seller: (closing) OK, now that we've agreed on a price I'll put a model TR300 aside for delivery next Friday.

Buyer: Hold on, don't rush me, I haven't made up my mind whether I'm ready to buy.

Seller: (still trying to close the deal) Would it be better if we scheduled a trial test next month. If it conforms to your requirements then we simply confirm the sale.

Buyer: (Showing irritation) Look, slow down will you. You still haven't shown the service support you provide and the terms of the warranty.

The best thing you can say about the closing techniques used here are that they brought out the customer's unresolved needs. However, in the process, the seller has unnecessarily antagonised the buyer.

A skilled sales negotiator would have dealt with all of the needs before trying to close the deal.

Seller: (checking all needs have been covered) Well, we seem to have covered a lot of ground. But before we go any further, are there any matters that possibly still concern you.

Buyer: Yes, you haven't gone over the terms of the warranty and what your "comprehensive backup service" really means.

Seller: Certainly, I'll go over that now. The warranty guarantees . . .

The seller has dealt with the other party's needs and concerns and the deal closes naturally, without any antagonism.

Seller: (closing) We have one model of the TR300 left in our showroom. Would you like us to set it aside for you for delivery next week.

Buyer: Yes, that'll be fine.

Common Closing Techniques

The two most popular and useful closing techniques are the summary close and concession close. They are popular for two reasons: they work and if used correctly don't antagonise the other side.

Summary Close

In the summary close you close the negotiation by:

- Summarising all that has been agreed to up till then.

- Emphasising the concessions you have made.

- Highlighting the benefits of agreeing to your proposals.

For example: "So far we've agreed on the base price for the TR300 machine of $476,000 plus an installation fee of $78,000. That's a reduction of 18% off our normal price for the machine, while the installation fee has been cut by 27.5%.

"Once installed the TR300 will speed up your invoice processing costs by 16%. It's much easier to use than your present system so training time will be much less. You've also mentioned how it will improve cash flow by speeding up payments.

"Given the progress we've made, it would be a shame if we now failed to reach agreement."

If the other party says, 'OK, I agree', and then puts a hand forward to confirm the deal, you've concluded the deal. Often they will say "Yes, but" and then go back over the issue or issues that remain outstanding.

Faced with this, you can move towards offering another concession to secure the close. For example: "If we agree on this outstanding issue are you saying we've got an agreement?"

If you can't afford to make a concession or want to demonstrate your commitment to the last offer, confirm your position. For example: "I'm sorry, but this is our final position. We can't give any more. There's simply nothing more in the kitty. We've conceded too much already. Look at all the concessions we've already made. All I can do is to agree to the deal as it stands now."

If this doesn't secure agreement, you now have to demonstrate how committed you are to your offer. As an act of commitment you might withdraw from the negotiation but leave the door open for a reopening of negotiations with a statement such as: "I think we've reached an impasse here. We simply can't afford to give any more. Look, why don't you call me back after you've had a chance to re-examine your position. I'm sure you'll find what we've offered is fair and generous."

The Concession Close

If you can't terminate negotiations with a summary close then you can try a concession close.

Most negotiators expect you to make a final concession to secure agreement. You should therefore always keep something of value back for the final trade.

If you've already signalled you're getting close to your limit by making your concessions progressively smaller, your final concession needn't be too large. Indeed, if you make too large a concession, your opponent may think there is still more for the taking and push you even harder.

The divisional head of a large government department was negotiating a special rate with a small, independently owned hotel for accommodation and meals for a weekend management team getaway.

The closing went:

Hotel: Look we've already cut our base rate by 40%. I believe that's extremely generous for a two day stay for a group of 12.

Buyer: Look, if you increase the rate to 50% and the accommodation and service is as good as we've heard, I will personally circulate all of the other divisional heads with a memo recommending your hotel.

The hotel agreed. It was in their long term interests to go along with the proposal. The government department got a great deal because of the way the divisional head imaginatively worded the final concession. The divisional head added value to the concession by *personally* promising to circulate a memo of recommendation. This is also a classic example of trading what is cheap for you in return for something much more valuable.

Splitting The Difference

An offer to split the difference will often close a deal. If, for example, you're $10,000 apart, you will often get a better response to an offer to split the difference than you will to a concession of $5000.

Splitting the difference works because it requires both sides to move and it appeals to our notions of equity and fairness.

However you cannot afford to split the difference unless you have positioned yourself properly, so that the split when it occurs is inside your limit.

Other Closes

Apart from the summary and concession closes there are dozens of others that are used.

The Weighing Close

One of my favourites is the weighing close. In this situation the other side seems keen on making a deal but still seems hesitant. To secure a close you say: "I appreciate you are very keen that any decision you make is the right one. So let's weigh up the reasons for hesitating against the reasons for proceeding with the agreement now."

You then take a piece of paper and draw a line down the middle. On one side you get the *other* party to list the reasons why they are hesitant. On the other side you list the reasons for proceeding now.

If you were trying to sell a new computer system the list might look like this:

Reasons For Hesitating	Reasons For Proceeding Now
We feel an obligation to our existing supplier.	Our three year warranties are the best in our field.
The price seems expensive.	24 hour on-site service.
	Increased processing speed will improve throughput by 27%.
	System is very easy to add to or change.

When writing up your reasons for proceeding now be careful not to exaggerate. For this to work it's important that the buyer sees it as a balanced assessment. Once the buyer has had a chance to weigh up the reasons, you can then say:

Seller: Is there anything we've missed out?
Buyer: Not that I can see.

Seller: What side makes the most sense?
Buyer: On balance you do seem to represent the best value for money. Let's proceed.

The Assumptive Close

A favourite close of many salespeople is the assumptive close. The seller asks a question that assumes the prospect will buy. If the buyer answers the question, he agrees to buy. Variations on these three are used all over the world:

- When will you want the microwave oven delivered?
- Do you want them in boxes of 10 or 50?
- When will you require us to complete the installation?

Used too early the assumptive close can be extremely irritating and generates replies such as: "Hold it! I didn't say I was going to buy it." If you do use it, make sure you've sorted out the other side's needs and they really are committed to proceeding with the deal.

Alternative Close

Another useful close is the alternative or the "either/or close". Instead of making a final "take it or leave it" stand you give the other side a choice. For example: "We can't afford to concede any more but we are prepared to offer you a choice. We can provide you with free delivery to all of your depots or if you use your own transport to pick up the goods we will discount the price by 2.5%. It's up to you. Which one best suits your needs?"

The Or Else Close

Desperate negotiators resort to the "or else" close. They present the other side with an ultimatum. "Either you meet our demands *or else* we will strike."

Threats such as these inevitably raise the temperature of a negotiation and often provoke the very resistance they are designed to overcome. Nobody likes being threatened.

Attitudes harden, and then it becomes a test of naked strength. If the other side thinks your threat is hot air, they may well call your bluff. And if you can't carry through your threat, your credibility evaporates and you're finished as a negotiator. Even if you have the power to carry through the threat and force the other side to cave in under duress, the benefits may well be short lived. Embittered opponents have a habit of biding their time and then seeking alternatives or even revenge.

When this happens, it's virtually impossible to generate the goodwill that's essential to achieve a win-win solution. The best you can hope for is a win-lose; the consequences may well be lose-lose.

Managing the Tension

The closing step is tense. Both sides are close to their limit as deadlines loom closer. Fear of deadlock increases. Patience is wearing thin, nerves break and mistakes are made. To escape the tension some negotiators simply walk away and abandon potentially good deals. Others become aggressive and belligerent, making ridiculous stands on minor issues of principle.

It is therefore imperative you keep your cool and stay in control.

Don't let deadline pressure get to you. Keep referring back to your time plan. Keep smiling and project confidence through your body language. Remember, most large concessions are conceded at the eleventh hour as negotiators feel their negotiating leverage crumble as their deadline looms ever closer.

Deadlocks

Don't get rattled by the fear of deadlock. The more time we invest in a negotiation, the more we have to lose from a breakdown. Some destructive negotiators play on this fear of deadlock by exaggerating the difficulties of reaching agreement. They create false deadlines, stage phoney walkouts and throw temper tantrums. Never fold under this sort of pressure. Call the other side's bluff and be prepared to deadlock and walk away if necessary. If the antics are staged, your opponent will soon find a face-saving way to resume talks.

Try to anticipate, avoid or sidestep last minute deadlocks. Be prepared to add extra tradable variables. The more issues there are, the more options there are to create win-win solutions. If you can't resolve the final issue, be prepared to link it to movement on one or several of the issues you've already settled.

Avoid provocative actions. If you happen to be an employer representative, there is little point in antagonising your opponents by calling them "industrial cowboys."

Change the time scale. If the negotiation is bogging down over minor short-term issues stress the long-term benefits of agreement. Often the short-term obstacles seem relatively minor when viewed against the potential long-term advantages for both sides.

If necessary change the negotiator. Sometimes a new face is needed to prevent or break deadlocks. A new person thinks differently, views the issues from a different perspective and can often generate movement in areas where others have failed.

Use a mediator. Sometimes an independent third party can be brought in to play the role of mediator. Mediators, who are commonly used in industrial relations and international diplomacy, have no formal power. Their task is to help the parties reach agreement between themselves. Mediation is a skilled job. Mediators have to be able to win acceptance from both sides. They need the ability to identify all the relevant issues and identify each side's priorities. Then they have to be able to nudge the two sides towards agreement by cajoling essential concessions from both sides and inventing acceptable proposals and solutions.

Keep questioning and listening. As negotiators lose their cool and control under the pressure of closing, they stop questioning and listening. Ironically this is the very time when these skills are most needed. Negotiators who continue questioning and listening find closing so much easier. Negotiations close naturally without the associated tension and antagonism.

Step Six:
Closing the Deal

Checkpoints:

- Decide at what point you want to stop trading.

- Assess whether it is the right time.

- Look out for body language cues.

- Listen for questions which indicate a readiness to close.

- Test the waters with a trial close.

- Start with a summary close.

- If necessary consider other possible closes.

- Guard against deadline pressures.

- Use body language to project a confident image.

- Try to anticipate and avoid last minute deadlocks.

- Consider changing the negotiator or using a mediator.

- Keep questioning and listening.

R-E-S-P-E-C-T

The seven steps to agreement

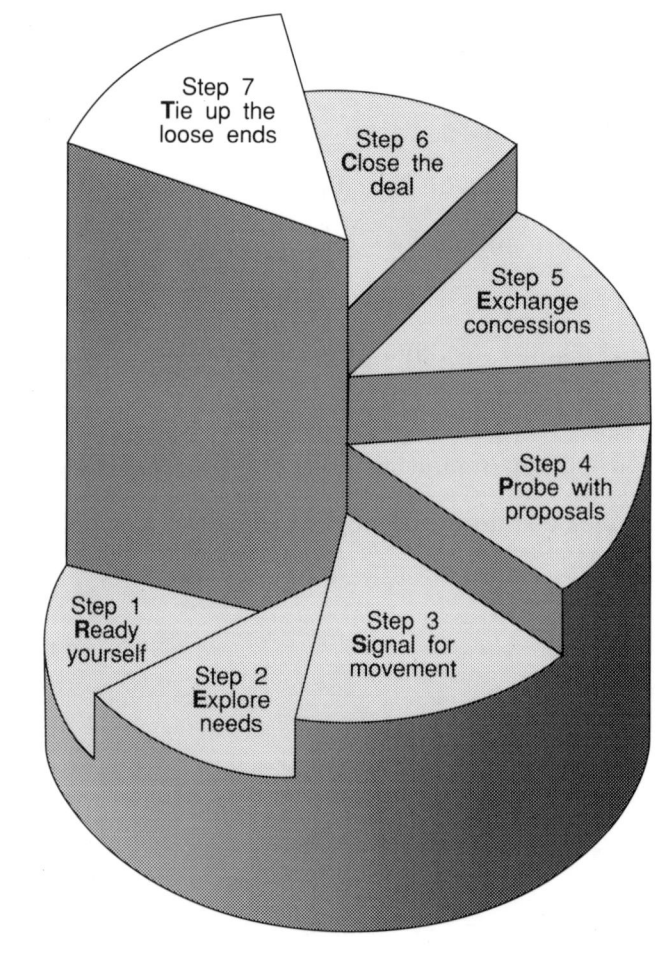

CHAPTER TEN

Step Seven:
Tying Up the Loose Ends

"For want of a nail the shoe was lost;
For want of a shoe the horse was lost;
For want of a rider the battle was lost;
All for the want of care about a horseshoe nail."

Benjamin Franklin

The red carpet rolled out. The champagne flowed as both parties congratulated each other on a great deal. Wall Street and the American media applauded the agreement. American Motors (AMC) and the Beijing Automotive Works had agreed to form a joint venture, the Beijing Jeep Company, to produce and sell jeeps in China. The Detroit *Free Press* hailed American Motors' move as "one of the shrewdest industrial strokes of the decade." The Chinese held 69% of the shares; the Americans controlled 31%.

According to the press release, the joint venture would first modernise the old Chinese jeep, the BJ212, used by the People's Liberation Army. This would be followed by a "new and second generation model" for sale in China and the Far East.

The Americans, however, never appreciated that the hazy language of the contract contained the seeds of future trouble. The agreement did not detail what type of new jeep would be built. There was no right for AMC to convert its Chinese earnings into dollars and there was no guarantee that the Chinese government would grant enough hard currency to buy key parts from the United States.

The joint venture had barely got off the ground in January 1984 when the two sides crossed swords over the jeep's design. The Americans wanted the design to be a copy of an AMC jeep so that parts could be swapped. The Chinese wanted a custom-made military jeep which their largest customer, the Chinese Army, could use. Such a jeep couldn't be made out of AMC parts. Both sides had glossed over this issue during the contract negotiations. Now it took months of intensive negotiations before the Chinese agreed to assemble AMC's newest product, the Cherokee Jeep, out of US imported kits. It would have cost over $1 billion to develop a new jeep and neither side could afford that.

Then, in late 1985, the Chinese government imposed tough foreign exchange restrictions. Without access to hard currency, the venture couldn't import the Cherokee part kits and couldn't exchange its local earnings into dollars, because domestic currency was not convertible.

For months Cherokee parts kits piled up in Detroit. To make matters worse, unpaid bills from Chinese government customers started piling up. By winter the Beijing Jeep Company was broke.

The Americans were close to abandoning the venture when the Chinese granted a major concession. They guaranteed Beijing Jeep Company enough foreign currency to import 12,500 Cherokee kits over four years. The Americans had originally planned for 5700 in 1986 and 40,000 annually by 1990.

The Chinese finally gave up their plans to build a new military jeep, and the long-envisaged "new second generation vehicle" was redefined as a Cherokee. Lastly the Chinese agreed to allow the venture to convert its Chinese earnings into foreign currency.

The Beijing Jeep Company was back in business. But at what cost? If both sides had not been carried away in the initial euphoria and had instead taken the time to tie up all the loose ends, the deal might have proceeded much more smoothly.[28]

Verifying What Has Been Agreed To

Don't ever leave a negotiation until you've gone back over every point in the agreement. Check your understanding against theirs and clear up any problems of interpretation. If you can't agree on what was said and agreed to at this stage, you're unlikely to do so later. Clarifying misunderstandings is much easier now as the memories of both sides are relatively fresh. Later, as memories fade, simple misunderstandings easily escalate into major differences as both sides start questioning each other's motives.

Put it in Writing

Once you've agreed on how to interpret the agreement, put it in writing. This need not be a formal contract; it might be a set of minutes, a facsimile or a memorandum of understanding.

Take Charge of the Writing

Always volunteer to do the writing. As the writer you're forced to think about the exact meaning of every word and clause. It really is surprising how much influence as a writer you exert in shaping the final agreement. Most of the time the other side will only concern themselves with a few key clauses. If, however, the other side drafts the agreement, force yourself to go through every clause. Question every ambiguity and be prepared to sit it out until they are all cleared up to your satisfaction. A few extra minutes now can later save thousands of dollars in expensive litigation.

If possible, write up the agreement before separating. If it's a complex or long contract which will have to be drafted later, draw up a memo of understanding summarising the undertakings of both parties. Then get both sides to initial it.

If there are potential legal fishhooks, engage professional help. If the other side has their legal experts along for the closing, so should you.

Write the Agreement in Plain Explicit Language

Write the agreement so it *cannot* possibly be misunderstood. Use simple familiar language; spell out precisely the obligations of both sides and avoid ambiguous words and phrases. The courts are clogged with disputes between parties who disagree over the precise meaning of words.

Planning for Future Differences

No agreement, however well drafted, can cover all the possible differences that might arise in the future. Most contracts include grievance and arbitration procedures but these should be used only as a last resort.

Win-win negotiators work hard to avoid legal solutions. They prefer to settle differences informally well before they require a legal solution.

If you anticipate there will be a need for regular meetings, plan for them early. Don't wait for disputes to break out before meeting the other side. Regular meetings allow you to solve problems while they are still small and manageable.

Reviewing the Performance

While your memory is still fresh enough to recall what happened, review your performance.

First, write down what happened in the order that it occurred. Second, go through each of the seven steps (RESPECT) and assess your performance. For example, as you evaluate your preparation ask questions such as:

- Did we identify the other side's interests correctly?
- Did we identify the key issues correctly?
- Did we make any wrong assumptions?
- How realistic was our time plan?
- Did we use the right strategy?

Finally, judge your overall performance by answering the big questions:

- How well did we do?
- Where could we have done better?
- What can we do to improve our performance in future negotiations?

Step Seven:
Tying Up the Loose Ends

Checkpoints:

- Verify what has been agreed to.

- Put the agreement in writing.

- Volunteer to do the writing.

- Write the agreement in plain explicit language.

- Question every ambiguity.

- Write up the agreement before separating.

- Plan for future differences.

- Review your performance.

CHAPTER ELEVEN

Building a Winning Relationship

"Industrial relations are like
sexual relations. It's better between two
consenting parties."

Lord Vic Feather

During the negotiations with the Arabs, Israeli stateswoman Golda Meir insisted on meeting her opponents face to face. A journalist suggested that this was not necessary.

"Even divorces are arranged without personal confrontation," he argued.

"I'm not interested in a divorce," retorted Mrs Meir. "I'm interested in a marriage."

Negotiations, like marriages, involve relationships. To work, both parties must be able to settle their differences. Roger Fisher and Scott Brown of the *Harvard Negotiation Project* define a successful working relationship as "one that is able to deal well with differences."[29]

A working relationship must be tough enough to handle differences caused by different values, different perceptions and different interests. It must be resilient enough to cope with fundamental disagreements, resilient enough to cope with outbursts of anger and resilient enough to keep the dialogue open – even when there seems little point in talking.

Differences rarely disappear magically. But if we keep the problem solving process open we dramatically increase the chances of working out a solution that satisfies both sides' interests.

The Golden Rules of Relationship Building

The essentials of a successful long-term working relationship can be boiled down to *reliability, rationality* and *receptivity*. Think of them as the three R's of relationship building.

Be Reliable

Reliability builds the trust and confidence that underpins a successful working relationship. Once you've proved "true to your word" your credibility soars and your words begin having a greater impact. Conversely we distrust unreliable people and discount everything they say or promise.

Reliable people are predictable. They don't upset us with nasty surprises which catch us unawares.

And reliable people consult us and keep us informed, before making major decisions which affect us.

Reliable people communicate clearly and precisely. When they make a commitment they spell it out precisely. For example, if they are promising to deliver your bedroom furniture, they say, "We *will* deliver it no later than Thursday afternoon." They carefully avoid making comments which can be easily misinterpreted such as, "We *should* be able to deliver the goods by Tuesday." Careless comments such as this can easily create false expectations and damage credibility.

Reliable people take *all* of their promises seriously. More importantly, they keep them – even when they seem small and trivial.

Reliable people are honest. Honesty is critical to a good working relationship. Reliable people do not practise deceit.

Honesty, however, does not require *full* disclosure. If, for example, one of your suppliers asks you for confidential costings, simply say, "I'm sorry but that is confidential information." That is much better than making up figures.

Be Rational

It's much easier to establish a good working relationship with someone who makes decisions based on reasons rather than emotion. Rational people don't get overwhelmed by emotion – they use reason and logic to build a case and keep their cool even when others lose theirs. Negotiators who remain rational invariably make fewer errors.

Emotions can never be entirely cut out of a negotiation. We all have emotional needs and satisfying them is an important part of most negotiations. Emotions such as affection and empathy can even improve relationships. Emotions such as fear and anger, however, block out logic and create barriers to understanding.

A negotiator must, therefore, deal openly with emotions which are damaging the relationship.

For example: "I appreciate you are angry. Let's see if we can get to the root of what is causing the problem." Acknowledging and talking about emotions allows reason to dominate. Once people are prepared to deal with emotions in a rational way the problem is under control.

Be Receptive

It's always easier to work with someone who is receptive to new ideas or suggestions and willing to listen and understand our needs and concerns. Because they are accessible, approachable and open-minded, we quickly forge bonds which make the settlement of differences that much easier.

Receptive people understand. They make the effort to understand the other side's needs, interests and concerns. They empathise, trying to see the problem through the other person's eyes.

Understanding requires regular two-way communication. We always appreciate it when other people consult us before making important decisions. Good communicators build rapport through active listening. When active listeners paraphrase contents and feelings, they demonstrate their understanding and interest.

Mutual Respect

To sum up, a successful working relationship is based on mutual *respect*. If you follow the advice offered in the seven steps of agreement (RESPECT) you will lay the foundation for a successful, long-term relationship. Remember, the art of negotiation is creating win-win agreements which last.

Psychological Traps

Advice such as this may seem like common sense. But, like much common sense, it isn't very commonly practised. Much of the difficulty we have in working collaboratively and building trust, understanding and commitment is psychological.

How often do both sides in a dispute quickly size each other up? One side thinks, "He looks like trouble. I've heard about him. There is no way he's going to put one over me. If he plays dirty then I'm prepared to play just as rough." Of course when the other person (who initially intended to be reasonable and cooperative) is confronted by such aggression, they respond in kind. Both sides become entrapped by a self fulfilling prophecy which quickly escalates into a full blown dispute.[30]

To show how easy it is to entrap others, I sometimes like to play a game called the Dollar Bill Auction. The game's inventor, Martin Shubik, a Yale economist, allegedly tested it on the Yale University cocktail party circuit. Try it. You'll make some money, but be prepared to lose a few friends.

Take a dollar bill from your pocket and announce you're prepared to auction it off to the highest bidder. There are three simple rules:

1. Bidding must be in multiples of 10 cents.

2. The highest bidder will win the dollar. However, the *second-highest bidder* must pay the auctioneer the amount of his or her losing bid. For example, if Penny bids 50 cents and Jerry has bid 40 cents; and the bidding stops at this point, the auctioneer will pay Penny 50 cents ($1 minus the amount bid) and Jerry, as the second highest bidder, pays the auctioneer 40 cents.

3. The auction ends when one minute passes without any new bids.

In a typical auction everyone bids furiously until they reach 50 or 60 cents. Then it begins to slow down. The number of bidders now usually falls until the two highest bids are $1.00 and 90 cents. At this point the two bidders ponder whether they should go on. Often the one who bids 90 cents will bid $1.10 and bidding erupts again. Then the bidding typically climbs to $4.00 or more.

The game often ends when one of the bidders sharply escalates the bidding by offering $5.00 to top a bid of say $4.10. The auctioneer then proceeds to collect $4.10 from the loser and $4 from the "winner". Of course there is no winner. The point of the game, once bidding passes $1.00, is to avoid losing – to save face. What starts out as a friendly contest quickly turns into a psychological struggle.

Emotional traps can be avoided if we are rational, reliable and receptive. Most disputes can be nipped in the bud by skilled negotiators who have a good working relationship. But beware. Once a conflict runs out of control and turns into a psychological struggle, the effect on the relationship may be terminal.

CHAPTER TWELVE

Power and Persuasion

*"All I want is a warm bed and
a kind word and unlimited power"*

Ashleigh Brilliant

B rilliant's words are the stuff of dictators and tyrants'
fantasies but negotiators should never similarly
indulge themselves. Negotiated agreements are, by
definition, voluntary. As long as you still can say no to a
proposal, you are in a negotiation. The moment you *absolutely* have to agree to a proposition, it is no longer a
negotiation.

Although the word "power" has all sorts of evil associations, power in itself is not good or bad. "Power," George
Bernard Shaw wrote, "does not corrupt men, but fools, if
they get into a position of power, corrupt power." You have
power over other negotiators to the extent that you can
induce them to do something they would otherwise not do.

Weak or unskilled negotiators often blame their poor
performances on a lack of power. "What could we do?" they
complain. "The other side held the upper hand." You can
recognise a good cardplayer by their ability to play a poor
hand. Top negotiators possess similar skills. Even when
they seemingly possess little power, they seem to be able to

get most of what they want. For them, power is largely a state of mind – a matter of perception.

Consider the problems an Eskimo trapper faces when he emerges from the Arctic darkness to trade his fox furs at the one and only trading post for hundreds of miles around. If ever a buyer enjoys a monopoly, it has to be the Arctic fur buyer. Yet the Eskimo knows just how to limit the power of the trader.

When a fur laden sledge carrying an Eskimo trapper, his wife and family emerges from the farthest wilderness on its six monthly trading mission, all the inhabitants of the village gather round to welcome them. The trapper and his wife enter the trader's house for a big feast. All the villagers come in too, listening and looking on. Peter Freuchen, a Norwegian fur trader, describes what follows in his *Book of the Eskimos*.

We discuss the weather, the hunting in the summer, the dogs. The only matter we don't talk about is foxes. Next day the same thing – eating, dancing, talking – and the next day and the next, until I for my part think that the hospitality has come to an end. Then I just casually ask the man whether he has caught any foxes this year.

"Me, foxes?" he answers. "Nothing doing. One is a poor hunter as far as that goes, but especially for foxes."

"Well," I say, "I'm sorry, because I'd like to have a few foxes just to send home to the white people's country when the ship arrives next summer."

"Oh!" the man yells out. The big, nice white man has made a mistake. "Oh, you don't know how unable I am to catch foxes."

"Well," I remark, "I saw a couple of bags out on the load which is now on the meat racks, and I thought they contained fox skins."

"Well," the man says, "maybe there's just a couple of skins in the bags, but we just use them to wipe the grease off our hands and other dirty things."

"Good!" I say. "But just the same I might like to have some of them. What about looking at them tomorrow?"

Next day comes, and after breakfast I again have to encourage the customer to show his merchandise. Now comes the big moment of the year. They bring in a couple of sacks, each containing some fifty blue fox skins, and they have beforehand assured themselves that the whole village is present to witness their triumph. As if they were being dragged to the gallows, they open the sacks and pour the contents out. Now it is my turn. I look at the skins, amazed, surprised and beaten.

"Well," I say, "as usual, those are the best skins in the year. I knew they would come from you; and they certainly did. Here is something I will have to mourn about for years, because I am unable to get those foxes."

The man raises his head, interested. "What did you say? Are they too poor for you to accept?"

"Oh no; not at all. Just the opposite. You will have to take every one of your skins back with you because I have nothing to pay with. The trading goods that came out this year were especially bad. We haven't got enough of them and they certainly aren't of a kind that can pay for such skins as yours."

"Pay!" yells the man at the top of his voice. "You don't think that I would show myself low enough to take any pay for those poor skins? I will feel myself happy if you'll accept them."

Finally I put in a question. "I am unable to pay for the skins but anxious to show my gratitude through my poor gifts. What could you be thinking of wanting in case I should be presumptuous enough to compare my unworthy goods to your valuable furs?"

He starts in. "What do I want! What do I want! Oh, I am a man without wishes. I don't know if I want anything."

It is then up to me. "Don't you want a gun?"

"A gun! A gun! Oh, a gun had been in my mind and in my dreams for a long, long time; but I, the man you listen to now, am a terrible hunter. Why should I have a gun?"

"Well, I will give you a gun. You need a knife, too, and you need some tools. And what more?"

Now that the big time is here he doesn't know what he wants. But I have the skins, so I invite the man, his wife, and his children to go into the store and look the things over. They get the key and go down to the store. They go in, closing the door carefully behind them, and spend the rest of the day going through everything.

Meantime, I get a chance to look these skins over and figure out my prices, and finally, in the evening when the couple comes back, the man has his wishes. He never tells what he wants, but he relates of what fine knives he saw, both those with the white handles and those with the brown, and the small ones with the point.

He goes on: "And then I looked at the files. My, what beautiful files! And I saw out there that you have axes."

He is interrupted by a sort of yelling or crying from the background. It is his wife, carefully instructed by him, who now breaks in complaining what a bold and fresh husband she has, keeping on asking like a beggar even when it has been proved to everybody that he has nothing to pay with. This, of course, only serves to cause me to protest that his skins are marvellous, unmatched so far, etc.

I turn to the wife. "What about you? Aren't you going to trade? Don't you want something?"

She blushes and looks for a place to hide. "Me? Certainly not! What should I want? Am I one who deserves anything? Oh, no; I have no wants, no wishes at all."

"But wasn't there something you would like?"

"I would like to have – oh, I happen to be without wishes; only those people who are worth something should have something."

"Well, but I just want you to take something with you."

And after several more excuses, she tells what she might like to have. A few needles. And she wanted some scissors, and she wanted thread. Maybe for the children some undershirts would be good, and some for herself; also combs. And "I would like to have a mirror, even though I, of course, will never look at myself in it."

The wife keeps on asking, and finally I have to stop her from asking for more. Meanwhile I have figured out how much they can have for each skin and write it down on a piece of paper, sending them out to my clerk, who now is in the store ready to deliver the goods. Now the clerk has his troubles out there while they are making their choice between the different cups, the different kettles, the guns and what not.

And now comes the end of the trading, where they show their smartness and prove what fine business people they are.

The man will come running in. "Oh, I'm so sorry; when I told you what my needs were I forgot to ask for tobacco. I'd like to have some tobacco."

"All right." I allow him the tobacco.

A few minutes after he will be back with his purchases.

"Well," he will say, "I saw a knife out there I would like to have instead of this one, though it will ruin my sleep to part with this one, too."

I let him have the knife.

The wife will be there. "There was also some red cloth."

Then the man comes again. "I have the whole time been thinking of a saw, but my tongue refused to pronounce the word."

I let him have the saw. And they keep on. The only way to stop them is to have lunch ready. And the deal is closed.

Next day the departure takes place. The dogs are harnessed up and attached to the sledge. But sure enough, he comes in at the last moment: "Oh, I forgot matches! Why didn't I mention a saw file! If I had only asked for a little more goods! Enough for a harpoon shaft!"

The smartest man is the man who remembers most. He gets a reputation amongst his countrymen. Of course the perfectly straight-minded man doesn't know about this and doesn't allow for it, but the seasoned trader keeps back four or five fox skins to make up for the forgettings and additional wishes.

When everything is loaded on and the woman and children placed on top of the sledge, the man gives a signal to the dogs to rise up and be alert. Then I come out with a package in my hand, giving the wife some tea and sugar, or whatever else I know she would like. Of course these things have been allowed for, too.[31]

The Eskimo showed all the skill of a master negotiator. From the start he involved the whole village in the negotiation. The villagers witnessed many of the proceedings. As a result the fur trader was always under public pressure to behave fairly and reasonably.

By playing the role of the reluctant seller the Eskimo forced the trader to publicly state how marvellous the furs were and how much he wanted them.

The Eskimo used time well. Throughout he displayed great patience; there was never any hint of desperation to sell.

Before they got down to the actual trading, the Eskimo and his family spent a whole day in the store sorting out their priorities. The actual trading was carefully orchestrated with his wife chiming in at opportune times. Then after the trading had supposedly ceased they were not averse to extracting a few last minute extras.

In short, the Eskimo understood the different ways power can be used, and exploited each of these to the fullest.

The Six Sources of Power

Social scientists have identified six sources of power: reward power, coercive power, legitimate power, information power, expert power and personal power.

Reward Power

Virtually every parent has used sweets, toys and other forms of bribes as a form of persuasion with their child. For children this is lollipop power. For sophisticated adults it is reward power. Teachers induce us to work harder for awards. Employers persuade us to work harder with higher wages, bonuses and profit sharing agreements. Anyone who can give or withhold a reward holds power. If you're buying a new house, you have the power to reward the salesperson with a commission or you can withhold the commission by refusing to buy.

The only way to protect yourself against the reward power the other negotiator has over you is to demonstrate your reluctance.

If you are buying a house, even if it happens to be the house of your dreams, be prepared to point out the faults. Let the seller know you're considering another similar site. Whatever you do, don't openly fall in love with the property. Your public display of affection could end up costing you dearly.

Coercive Power

Coercive power is the opposite to reward power. Any person or institution who has the power to punish or take something away from you holds coercive power.

A sales manager cuts his salesman's pay for failing to meet the year's target. An executive fires his secretary for failing to cut down on the number of typing mistakes. A mother berates her child for failing to clean up the backyard. A supplier imposes a penalty charge on an overdue account. A bank forecloses on a loan.

In 1988, when Walt Disney executives were negotiating to buy Wrather Corporation, owners of the Disneyland Hotel, they threatened to sharply increase the fees for the use of the monorail which links the hotel to the Disney theme park. According to *Fortune* magazine, "this gun-to-the-head tactic forced Wrather to sell the company for less than what Wrather's top executives thought it was worth."[32]

Coercive power should not be thought of as necessarily evil or immoral.

A parent or school which no longer had the power to discipline would be as toothless as an employer who lacked the power to fire.

Because of its negative connotations, however, coercive power must be exercised with great discretion, especially where goodwill is involved.

Following Germany's defeat in the first World War, a delegation of the German forces went to the French commander, Marshal Foch, to ask for armistice terms. Foch picked up a paper from his desk and read out a list of conditions.

"But — there must be some mistake," the leader of the German delegation stuttered in disbelief. "No civilised nation could ever impose such terms on another."

"I am very glad to hear you say so," replied Foch. "No, gentlemen, these are not our terms. These are the terms a German commander imposed on one of our cities, Lille, when it was surrendered to you."

When you use coercive power, always carefully think through the long-term effects. Coercive power can easily damage a relationship.

To counter coercive power, you must overcome your fears and be prepared to stand up for what you feel is right. Don't allow the fear of punishment to cloud your judgement. Insist that any proposal you make be treated on its own merit.

Legitimate Power

Imagine you've volunteered to take part in an experiment on the study of memory with Professor Stanley Milgram at Yale University.

When you arrive at the laboratory suite, you are met by a stern faced researcher dressed in a grey lab coat. The other person you meet is a likeable, mild mannered, middle aged accountant.

The researcher explains the experiment is about how punishment affects learning. After drawing lots, you end up playing the part of the teacher, the accountant will play learner. The accountant is given a long list of pairs of words to memorise.

You then go into a neighbouring room. The learner is strapped into an "electric chair" type construction. An electrode is attached to the learner's wrist. Electrode paste is also applied to "avoid blisters and burns." The researcher tells you the electrode connects to a shock generator unit located in an adjacent room.

By now you're feeling nervous. You go into the room with the shock generator. It has 30 lever switches, each marked between 15 and 450 volts. The switches are grouped under labels, Slight Shock, Moderate Shock, Strong Shock, Very Strong Shock, Intense Shock, Extreme Intensity Shock and Danger: Severe Shock. The last two switches are simply labelled XXX.

The researcher instructs you, "Administer a shock to the learner every time he gives a wrong answer to a question.

And if he gives another wrong answer move one notch higher on the shock generator." The shocks, the researcher tells you, can be very painful and demonstrates it by inflicting a 45 volt shock on you – just to prove the equipment is working.

The first part of the test seems relatively harmless. There is the odd mistake but the shocks seem tolerable. Then the mistakes begin piling up and the voltages rise sharply. At 120 volts the learner shouts, "Experimenter, get me out of here! I don't want to be in the experiment any more! I refuse to go on!" At 180 volts he screams, "I can't stand the pain" and by 270 volts the scream is of agonizing pain. When the 300 volt barrier is passed the learner thumps the wall.

Whenever you declare you want to stop the shock, the experimenter commands you to continue.

What would you really do faced with this situation? Would you defy the experimenter and refuse to continue inflicting the shocks? How high would you go before stopping?

Before the experiment started, Milgram asked groups of psychiatrists, students and middle class adults how many subjects would administer the maximum shock of 450 volts. The vast majority predicted between 1 to 4%.

In stark contrast, Milgram found huge numbers – 62 per cent in fact – of the volunteer "teachers" were prepared to administer the maximum shock of 450 volts. (Please note, the shocks were never actually administered. Milgram's learners were actors.)

What explains these alarming findings? Were the volunteer teachers an unrepresentative bunch of twisted sadists? No. Personality tests and repeat experiments confirmed Milgram's subjects were a typical bunch of ordinary citizens.

What then caused them to behave in such horrifying ways? "It has to do," Milgram says, "with a deep seated sense of duty to authority within us all." Despite the fact that virtually all of the subjects wanted to defy the wishes of the experimenter, when it came to the crunch they couldn't bring themselves to defy the wishes of the boss of the study – the lab coated researcher. The lab coat and all the surrounding circumstances vested the experimenter with legitimate power.

And adults will go to extraordinary lengths to obey a command from a legitimate authority.[33]

We shouldn't be too surprised by this finding. If we didn't go along most of the time with those who hold legitimate power – police, judges, bosses – society would collapse into chaos.

When we vest someone with a title, office or a role we confer on them legitimate power. The English Monarchy may not have much coercive power left but it still holds substantial legitimate power. Soldiers follow their officers' orders without question because they have been trained that it is necessary or "legitimate" for them to do so. Title-holders surround themselves with trappings and symbols to emphasise the power of the position. As executives climb the corporate ladder, offices get larger, furnishings get more luxurious and cars turn into limousines.

Be prepared to challenge legitimate power when it is being used unreasonably against you. Don't be intimidated or hypnotised by titles, positions or offices, or the trappings that go with them. American businessman and diplomat Joseph Kennedy advised, "Whenever you're sitting across from some important person, always picture him sitting there in a suit of red underwear." That, he claimed, was the way he "always operated in business."

Information Power

The year: 1912. Teddy Roosevelt was nearing the climax of a hard fought presidential campaign. The final push was a whistlestop tour through middle America. At each stop Roosevelt planned to deliver an inspiring address and hand out thousands of pamphlets. On the cover of each pamphlet was an imposing Presidential portrait; inside was a rousing speech. Hopefully, these would win over vital undecided voters.

The final tour was about to begin when a campaign worker noticed a small printed notice on each photo: Moffett Studios – Chicago. The photograph was copyright and no one had obtained a clearance from Moffett.

Unauthorised use of the photo could cost a dollar for each pamphlet distributed. The prospect of a three million dollar bill sent a chill through the campaign workers. They simply couldn't afford it. The pamphlets were a crucial part of the re-election strategy. If they went ahead without Moffett's permission and were caught out, they'd be branded law-breakers and be liable for a small fortune.

The campaign workers concluded they had no choice; they had to negotiate with Moffett, and there was no time to lose.

You can imagine how they felt. Moffett seemingly had them over a barrel.

Dejected, they sought campaign manager George Perkins's help. Perkins immediately instructed his typist to cable Moffett.

"We are planning to distribute many pamphlets with Roosevelt's picture on the cover. It will be great publicity for the studio whose photograph we use. How much will you pay us to use yours?"

The reply soon came back. "We've never done this before, but under the circumstances, we'd be pleased to offer you $250."

Legend has it Perkins accepted without asking for more.[34]

Perkins understood the power of information; the critical role it plays in shaping a negotiation. By selectively controlling the flow of information to Moffett, Perkins created the illusion he held the upper hand.

Information power lies at the heart of the bargaining process. In even the simplest of negotiations, both parties take a position, then present facts, arguments, data and other information to support that position. Both sides then use information to get the other side to modify their position until there is enough common ground to reach a mutually satisfactory settlement.

To guard against information being manipulated or concealed, you must do your homework. The more information you have, the more power you have. It's that simple.

Expert Power

Imagine your family has moved to a new neighbourhood where they have been plagued by a rash of common illnesses. Lots of your neighbours suffer from the same ailments. All you can put it down to is pollution from a local chemical factory.

You consult a lawyer who says to succeed in a court case against the chemical plant you will have to establish a direct link between low-level toxins and specific illnesses. This has proved virtually impossible. However you might stand a chance if you hire an expert in this area – who has been able to persuade juries that pollution can suppress the immune system. Pollution can then be blamed for a wide range of common ailments.

This particular theory is promoted by a small group of experts who call themselves clinical ecologists, practitioners of environmental medicine and immunologists. The American Academy of Allergy and Immunology and the California Medical Association rejects the theory. But

American juries have awarded damages to claimants amounting to millions of dollars based on evidence presented by so-called experts in this area.[35]

Expert power is a special form of information power. Information from an expert is much more credible, more persuasive.

Experts typically establish their authority by showing us their credentials – their qualifications. Doctors, dentists, lawyers hang their qualifications on their office walls to impress us.

Experts demonstrate their expert knowledge by being able to cite lots of facts and figures and by proving their mastery of the subject by being able to draw on information that is not commonly known. Experts enhance their expertise by writing articles and books. Being referred to or quoted on paper suggests expert status.

If you hold expertise in your area, be prepared to demonstrate it. If you don't and the costs warrant it, enlist the aid of an expert to support you. Experts are more convincing. The other side's non-experts tend to defer to your expert by being less aggressive and less dogmatic.

To inoculate yourself against expert power, be especially thorough in your homework and remember Emerson's dictum "nothing so astonishes men so much as common sense and plain dealing."

Personal Power

As a rule we prefer to agree to requests from people we know and like.

Joe Girard, whom the Guiness Book of Records called the world's greatest car salesman, averaged more than five car and truck sales every day he worked. He used a very simple sales formula. He offered his customers just two things: a fair price and someone they like to buy from. "And that's it," he claimed in an interview. "Finding the salesman they like, plus the price; put them both together and you get a deal."[36]

Joe Girard obviously had special personal qualities that appealed to his customers. Those personal qualities which give one person the ability to influence another are called *personal* power or *referent* power.

Such qualities might include honesty, openness, integrity, friendliness, charm. The list is endless because different qualities influence different people. The qualities can be physical. Handsome men and beautiful women usually find it easier to make friends and influence others.

Charismatic personalities are a very select group of personal power holders such as Martin Luther King and Mahatma Gandhi who possess a unique mix of personal characteristics which enables them to influence large numbers of people.

While few possess the charisma of a King or Gandhi, we can influence those who identify and relate with us. Commonly this flows out of a relationship. Typically we are attracted to those who share similar attitudes, values and interests. On the other hand we find it much harder to relate to or influence people with whom we have little in common.

To increase our personal power we have to improve our relationship building skills. To protect ourselves against the misuse of personal power we must, from time to time, be willing to test the relationship.

If, for example, you felt a close neighbour was taking advantage of your relationship by continually seeking "free" legal advice, you have little choice but to raise your concern directly with him. Say: "Peter, I don't mind giving you the odd piece of neighbourly advice, but most of these matters have complex legal ramifications which I'd rather deal with as part of a normal lawyer-client relationship. Is it possible for you to come down to my office tomorrow?"

Use your understanding of the six sources of power to increase your leverage.

Top negotiators draw on all six sources to maximize their power.

One of the most effective General Managers I know uses productivity bonuses to encourage staff to work harder (reward power). Although she rarely has to do it, she weeds out non performers who fail to meet minimum standards (coercive power). She enjoys the complete support of her board to carry out any decisions (legitimate power). Even as a junior manager, her staff never grumbled at the 12 to 16 hours per day they had to work to achieve her ambitious targets (personal power). Her mastery of software engineering still commands the respect of the technical staff (expert power), while in meetings she is always well briefed (information power).

CHAPTER THIRTEEN

Planning Your Strategy

*"Never go into a negotiation
without knowing what you want to achieve and
how you intend to accomplish it."*

In a negotiation your strategy is your game plan or basic approach. The major task in this book has been to show how to negotiate favourable deals which last. To get what *you* want from others, the best approach is usually to help them get what *they* want. Agreements which leave both sides satisfied work better because both parties are committed to holding up their side of the agreement.

Effective negotiators therefore always look out for opportunities to turn win-lose confrontations into win-win collaborations.

When Israel and Egypt started negotiations to draw up a peace treaty following the Six Day War of 1967 and Yom Kippur War of 1973, it seemed their interests were in direct conflict. Israel wanted to keep part of the Sinai Peninsula which it had captured from the Egyptians in 1967. Egypt, on the other hand, wanted all of her territory returned.

As neither side were prepared to move an inch the parties deadlocked in a classic win-lose confrontation.

During the Camp David peace talks held in late 1978, the two sides, with the help of the Americans, reexamined their interests. The Israelis' fundamental interest was security. They wanted to keep the Sinai so they could use it as a buffer zone to buy extra time in case of an Egyptian attack across their common border. The Egyptians' fundamental interest was sovereignty; the Sinai had been part of Egypt for centuries.

At Camp David, Egypt's President Sadat and Israel's Prime Minister Begin agreed to a solution which satisfied Israel's need for security and Egypt's demand for sovereignty. The Egyptians agreed to demilitarise large parts of the Sinai. In exchange the Israelis returned the Sinai to Egyptian rule.[37]

By discussing their needs, reconciling their interests and improving their relationship, both sides ended up better off.

However it would be naive and irresponsible to claim goodwill and skill can turn every win-lose contest into a win-win collaboration. They can't. Sometimes no amount of problem solving and discussion of needs can get around the problem that the size of the pie we are negotiating over is fixed. If we can't enlarge it, whatever share you get will be at my expense. The best we can hope for is a tolerable compromise.

We also have to negotiate with hardliners who don't care about our needs. For them, negotiation always has been — and always will be — a contest of wills.

Effective negotiators, of necessity, therefore, have to be "situational" negotiators; they are prepared to adapt their strategy to fit the situation. When assessing what approach to use, they consider five key questions:

- Is there going to be a continuing relationship?
- What are the relative strengths of the parties?
- How much trust exists?
- What do we know about the personality and style of the other side?
- How much time is available?

1. Is there going to be a continuing relationship?

In a one-off deal where you never expect to meet the other side again, the incentives to be open and behave reasonably are less than in a situation where you know you have to, or want to, do business with the other party again.

Most people, for example, are more open and reasonable when selling a car to a friend or relation than they are when selling the same car to a stranger whom they never expect to meet again.

Even the most committed win-win collaborative negotiators turn into hard competitive bargainers when they become tourists in the markets of Hong Kong or Mexico.

2. What are the relative strengths of the parties?

The difference in strength between the two parties, or the *balance of power* as some negotiators call it, can strongly influence the approach.

If Barrington Industries happen to be the sole supplier of a basic component essential to the success of your business, then they are in a strong position to adopt a tough line in any negotiations with you. It is, therefore, in your interests to cultivate an harmonious working relationship.

If, on the other hand, you can choose from numerous suppliers, then you are in a much stronger position and can afford to adopt a much more competitive approach.

3. How much trust exists?

A win-win strategy requires a high degree of trust and openness. This usually takes time.

At times you will also have to negotiate with people who have proven themselves untrustworthy. With untrustworthy or unreliable clients you have little choice but to adopt a tougher, less open, approach.

4. What do we know about the personality and style of the other side?

Like it or not, there are negotiators who simply work for their own interests, view negotiation as a power struggle and care little for the needs of the other side. They are ruthlessly competitive, abrasive, are essentially untrusting and are prepared to win at any cost. With such negotiators, your approach has to be more competitive and less reliant on trust than it is with a negotiator who uses a cooperative style.

Highly cooperative negotiators, on the other hand, are sensitive to the needs of the other side. They emphasise problem solving, "aim to maximise joint gains; focus on common interests, not differences; are non-confrontational, non-argumentative, and apply standards of 'fairness', 'commonsense' and 'reasonableness'."[38]

Cooperative negotiators often worry that they risk being exploited by competitive opponents. While this sometimes happens, you quickly learn to adjust your style. Similarly, competitive negotiators who lose business because of their aggressive style soon learn to adapt.

5. How much time is available?

Time is a key strategic variable. Negotiators under time pressure lower their aspirations and concede more. The side with the time advantage can therefore adopt a tougher, more competitive approach.

While this can result in a short term victory, the long term consequences can be costly. Highly competitive tactics undermine the trust and goodwill needed to build a long-term working relationship which needs time and nurturing to develop.

In short, to succeed as a negotiator you have to be flexible. Your strategy depends on the circumstances and issues of the negotiation. Nevertheless, don't forget that your goal should be to resolve the conflict in a way that leaves both sides satisfied and committed.

CHAPTER FOURTEEN

Choosing the Right Tactics

"Send two dozen roses to
Room 424 and put 'Emily, I love you' on the
back of the bill."

Groucho Marx

actics are the gambits and ploys you use to achieve
your strategy. Negotiation tactics have two main
objectives:

- To strengthen your position in the other party's eyes.
- To alter the other party's view of their own position.

The more you can achieve these objectives, the more
likely the deal will suit you better. This does not mean that
your opponent will necessarily be worse off. You may both
win from a settlement which is different from either of your
original proposals.[39]

There are hundreds of tactics. What follows is an A to Z
summary of 18 of the most common. Most tactics you'll come
across will be variations on these. Even if you would never
dream of using some of these tactics, you need to be able to
recognise and counter them.

Add-On

The add-on tactic consists of adding unexpected extras on to the quoted terms for a deal. Merchants use it to boost their prices. You purchase a washing machine which, on the price tag says $895 (it includes free installation and 12 months free credit). You assume this is the full price.

When you analyze the bill it actually comes to $1055. The add-ons include $30 for delivery, $85 for plumbing fittings and a $45 administration charge for the so called free credit.

Counter: Exercise caution before you agree to the deal and check out exactly what is included in the price before you agree to buy. If there are extras, push for them to be included in the original price.

The Budget Limitation

Imagine you've just submitted a bid to redesign and renovate a client's premises for $68,000. Your client says "I like your proposal, but I'm afraid all I've got is $55,000."

Your client is using the budget limitation or *bogey* tactic as it is sometimes called. You can either cut your price or come up with alternatives.

The bogey tactic is entirely ethical. A legitimate budget limitation or bogey encourages the seller to cut her price and redesign her package to solve the buyer's budget problems.

Counter: You should anticipate the bogey by preparing alternative packages in advance. However you should also always be prepared to resell the value of your original proposal.

For example: "I appreciate your budget can't stretch to meet our original proposal. Would you be prepared to consider some lower cost componentry. If you were prepared to change your specification to allow us to use our standard components, then I'm sure we can meet your budget better than anyone else."

Sometimes you can get around the budget limitation by changing the time frame for payments. You might allow the client to pay 60% of the cost this budget period and delay the rest until the next budget period.

Sometimes you can turn a budget restriction into a creative opportunity to extract other concessions.

For example: I think we could meet your budget if:

- you will agree to purchase all your supplies from us for the next two years.
- you will also grant us the contract for the book-keeping services as well.
- you will use your transport to pick up the equipment.
- you order in minimum lots of six dozen.
- we can put off the training programmes until late July.

Escalation

Escalation is one of the most effective negotiation pressure tactics used. Sometimes it's ethical, sometimes it's not. It all depends upon the circumstances and the motives of the user.

You shop around for a 35mm camera, set of lens and accessories, and eventually find a dealer who, after a lengthy bargaining session, offers to sell you the complete kit for $800. You return the next day to pay for it when the seller says, "I'm sorry but the price we agreed to yesterday is too low. We simply can't afford to offer it to you at that price, the best we can do is $900." What do you do? Walk away? Many people don't. They've invested too much time in the deal and it's too much trouble negotiating another deal with another company, so they agree to the "escalated price".

Escalation can help a seller protect their original position.

Fyfson Communications receives an estimate for $420,000 for building maintenance services. Evan Peterson, Fyfson's building manager, is convinced that he can reduce the price to $350,000. When the negotiations begin, however, the building maintenance firm's manager opens with an apology that the original figure was the result of a miscalculation. He needs $475,000 to provide the level of service required and supports the figure with a detailed breakdown of his costings.

Evan isn't convinced the original figure was in error, but it certainly scuttles his hopes for a $350,000 package. In fact he is delighted when the final figure is settled at $420,000.

Counter: The only effective way to deal with the escalation is to test it by calling the other side's bluff. First, call for convincing evidence that the escalation is justified. If it isn't forthcoming, walk away.

Lack of Authority

You negotiate a deal with someone you think has full authority to make the deal or make concessions. You're just about to close the agreement when the other side says, "I have to take this to my manager for approval." Commonly this leads to another round of negotiating and calls for further concessions.

Counter: The best defence is to check before you start negotiating whether the negotiator has full authority to settle. If your contact hasn't, try to negotiate with the real decision maker. If that's not possible, build some padding into your offer in anticipation of another round of concessions.

Finally, you always have the right to withdraw or change your concessions. Say: "I didn't appreciate our agreement needed further approval, but that's okay. We treat this agreement as a statement of intent. While your manager checks it out, we'll also review it for possible changes."

Misleading Information

Sometimes negotiators deliberately mislead the other side as to their true needs, interests and priorities. They know how valuable it is to know the other party's wants, deadlines and resources. They therefore deliberately try to confuse the other party by creating straw issues and leading the other party down false trails.

In a commercial negotiation over a complex contract, one party spends most of the time discussing clause 16 to divert the other party's attention from their real concern, clause 27.

A trade union produces claims for new disciplinary procedures, demands for limitations on overtime and calls for changes in the company health scheme, and tacks them on to the annual wage and conditions claim as red herrings to distract the company from their true priority – extended union coverage.

Counter: Thorough preparation is the best defence against misleading information. Check out all information which might affect the negotiation. Effective questioning, plus a careful analysis of the other side's pattern of concession, will also help you clarify their true needs and priorities.

Outrageous Initial Demand

Your opponent begins by making an outrageous initial demand, much more than you ever contemplated. This shock tactic is designed to get you to make a much higher offer than you ever imagined possible. By taking an extreme position he causes you to move closer to his ideal position.

Counter: Almost always the outrageous initial demand is a bluff. Above all, don't get rattled by the demand. Stick with your original offer, carefully explaining all the benefits.

Nibble

I have a friend who never buys a suit without nibbling for a tie or belt. He waits for the salesperson to start writing out the sales docket, then says, "You'll throw in a free tie, won't you?" The tactic invariably works. The other party is already committed to the close, and is unwilling to risk the whole deal for the sake of a nibble which is so tiny compared to the rest of the deal.

Nibbling is widespread. Buyers nibble by paying invoices late, by claiming rebates they are not entitled to and asking for extra services to be provided for nothing. Sellers nibble by adding on unexpected extra charges, by delivering slightly more than ordered or by not providing promised services.

Counter: If you are buying, find out exactly what you are buying before you close the deal. If you are selling:

- Plead lack of authority to grant the extras.
- Publish a price list that specifies the extra charges for all extras and details your firm's policies. (The written word always has more authority than the spoken word.)
- Turn the nibbler's request down politely. Most nibblers are only having you on.
- Anticipate the nibble by including it in your original price.

Linking

In any negotiation where there are a number of issues, you have to decide whether to deal with each issue on its own, as a separate negotiation in its own right, or whether to link them together and treat them as part of a single package.

By linking the issues you increase the variables and the range of possibilities. You can trade movement on one issue against movement on another.

Linking in complex negotiations calls for more skill. Lots more variables have to be kept under control. Linking favours the well prepared.

Sometimes in a very complex negotiation with a lot of contentious issues, it can pay to separate and agree on a number of small issues· first to create a feeling of momentum.

Reverse Auction

The reverse auction is one of the most fiercely competitive tactics used in negotiations.

Let's say you have three bids or tenders for the installation of a new heating system. You intend to give the job to the lowest bid, but when all the bids come in you find each one is a little different in terms, fittings and warranties.

You therefore invite all the bidders to your office and play one off against the other in a reverse auction. You selectively quote from each of their bids, being careful to stress aspects where their rivals are better and where they need to improve. The weaknesses in the three systems are also exposed as each of the rivals points out the weaknesses of the others.

You finally give the job to the one offering the best package.

The reverse auction works because it intensifies the competitive process. However, most participants hate it. If you value a good working relationship with your supplier, don't use it.

Counter: If you are faced with an offer to rebid, decline it on the grounds it is unethical. If you have to rebid, make your bid last, and make only one bid.

Salami

Salami comes in thin slices. That's how negotiators use the salami tactic. They achieve what they want by going after a slice at a time. A union opens with a request for a retraining allowance in addition to the standard lay off payments for workers whose skills have been made obsolete by technological changes. They then extend it one slice at a time to cover other groups such as the over 40s who will find it difficult to get replacement jobs until eventually it covers everyone.

Counter: To protect yourself against the salami, tie up every salami concession with detailed restrictions and exclusions. Don't just spell out what it covers, state also what it doesn't apply to. This makes it much tougher for the salami to be extended later.

Split the Difference

Splitting the difference is a quick way of reaching agreement. Two sides lock on two positions. They are prepared to offer $1000, you are prepared to offer $600. By splitting the difference you jointly agree on $800.

Splitting the difference is seductive, it seems fair and reasonable. Sometimes it is, but sometimes it isn't, especially if you can't afford to split the difference or the split is closer to their limit than to yours.

Counter: If you can't afford to split the difference, say so. Offer a different split, "I can't afford 50-50, but I will consider 40-60."

Your best protection against splitting the difference is to start with a high opening offer and concede slowly so when a call to split the difference occurs the split will favour you.

Take It or Leave It

In most negotiations there comes a point when one side says, "That's my final offer." They might even aggressively add, "It's up to you, take it or leave it."

"Take it or leave it" used aggressively arouses great hostility. Nobody likes being threatened with an ultimatum. Nevertheless take it or leave it tactics, albeit in politer forms, are used on us daily without causing offence. Whenever, for instance, we buy any good or service with a fixed price tag we are in effect being told to take it or leave it.

Counter: Skilled negotiators have a number of ways of getting around the "take it or leave it."

They test the "take it or leave it" by changing the nature of the proposed package. For example, "We could accept your final offer, if you were prepared to pick up the fittings at our factory."

They restate the advantages of accepting their package and repeat the points on which mutual agreement has already been reached. Sometimes they carry on the negotiation as though they never heard it. Other times they walk out, leaving the door open for a reopening of talks without loss of face. For example, "We can't accept your final offer, I'm afraid we simply can't afford it. If, however, you can find a way to reconsider your final offer, then please call us."

Tough Guy, Nice Guy

This act – and it is an act – is a variation of the good cop, bad cop interrogation routine played out in dozens of movies and TV shows.

The first interrogator – the bad cop – threatens to bully and bludgeon the prisoner into submission. When the prisoner fails to crack, the bad cop withdraws and the good cop takes over. The good cop adopts a much softer approach. He offers a cigarette, a drink, is much more conciliatory and apologises for his colleague's behaviour. Nevertheless he still advises the prisoner to confess. A confession, he explains, will serve everyone's interest and enable him to secure a better deal for the prisoner.

In commercial negotiations the tough guy adopts a competitive, uncompromising position. In a typical sales negotiation she declares, "We're not prepared to pay a cent above $2.80 a unit and they have to be delivered within five days of ordering." The other negotiator adopts a softer, more cooperative, compromising stance. "Come on Carol, don't be unreasonable, Peter has always served us well over the years. He has always supported us when we've been caught short. He also has to make a living. Surely we can go to $3.15 and give him 10 days to deliver."

If it all goes to plan, the salesperson will grab the good guy's offer even though it is well below what is realistic.

Counter: The best defence is to recognise the tactic. The tough guy and the nice guy – whether men or women – are a team. They are a duet. Once you appreciate this fact, it's much easier to defend your original proposal as fair and reasonable.

What If

Negotiators use the "what if" tactic to dig information out of the other side.

Imagine you want to purchase 2000 rolls of plastic. You will gain valuable information on the other side's costings and economies of scale if you also ask the supplier for prices for 500, 2000 and 5000 rolls. You will gain even more information if you pose further hypothetical questions such as:

- *What if* we were to change the specification?
- *What if* we allow you to deliver in your quiet period?
- *What if* we were to supply the dies for manufacture?
- *What if* we picked up the rolls at your plant?

A shrewd analyst can use information such as this to calculate the other side's costs of production and their likely bottom line. Some buyers find out the price for 10,000 items when they only want 1000 and then order the 1000 at the 10,000 price. When the seller protests, the buyer claims this is the first of a series of orders which will more than justify the volume discount.

Counter: When the other party starts asking "what if", you need to be very careful. Carefully word your answers so you don't give away any more than necessary. If the other side uses the information to demand a better price, you must be prepared to defend your original offer.

What's Your Rock Bottom Price?

This is another pressure tactic most commonly used by buyers. A buyer facing an inexperienced seller says, "Look, I don't have time to haggle. What is your rock bottom price?" This pressurises the seller into making a low opening offer at which point serious negotiations begin.

Counter: Never provide a rock bottom price. Stick with your intended opening offer. Retake the initiative by replying, "Well, I think a *fair* price would be $87,000". This becomes the starting figure for the negotiation.

What's Your Cost Breakdown?

Very often when a proposal is put up to provide goods or services the buyer will ask for a more detailed cost breakdown. On the face of it this seems a reasonable request. But if you give out the information, the buyer has a lever to extract a better price.

For example, a designer quotes $14,800 to design, layout and typeset a report. The client asked for a detailed breakdown of the costings. The client then seeks bids from various typesetters and uses the lowest one to force the designer to cut the typesetting part of the bill by $1100. This is in spite of the fact that the total package price is already cheaper by $2200 than that offered by any other designer.

Counter: In most cases you don't have to provide cost breakdowns. If you are asked, say, "I'm sorry but it's company policy to keep costings confidential. I'm sure you can appreciate our competitors would love to know how we can remain competitive and still provide such a good service."

Yes But

Negotiators commonly extract valuable last minute concessions with the "yes but" tactic.

You are about to close the deal when they say *"Yes,* that's fine, we agree, *but* there is a small point in clause 12 that needs clearing up." You concede on clause 12 when they identify another reservation, this time it's clause 32.

Counter: Before dealing with the first "yes but" check there are no other outstanding items of concern. Then say, "I'm prepared to consider these new points but only if you're prepared to accept some changes in the areas we've all already agreed on."

You've Got to Do Better Than That

This must be one of the most common tactics. For some professional buyers "you've got to do better than that" is an automatic reflex to any sales proposal. They assume there is a margin built into any price proposal and this is the quickest way to get to the bottom line.

One of the toughest General Managers I've ever met uses a variation on this with staff whenever they submit production schedules or budgets. It's amazing how quickly his staff discover ways of shortening their schedules or trimming their budget.

Counter: Once recognised, this tactic can be beaten by building an extra cushion into the price, schedule or budget.

CHAPTER FIFTEEN

The Sixteen Critical Success Factors

*"The winds and waves
are always on the side of the
ablest navigators."*

Edward Gibbon

Of all the factors that contribute to negotiation success there are 16 critical ones. Concentrate on these and you too will become a master negotiator.

1. Prepare thoroughly. Thorough preparation is often the difference between success and failure. Time spent on homework repays itself a thousand times.

2. Focus on interests rather than positions. The art of negotiation lies in reconciling interests – yours and theirs.

3. Use a BATNA rather than a bottom line. A BATNA (*Best Alternative To A Negotiated Agreement*) provides protection, flexibility and encourages imaginative problem solving.

4. Know your priorities. Successful negotiators value every issue and rank their priorities in order of importance. They trade off their low priorities in order to achieve their top priorities.

5. Make time work for you. Top negotiators rarely get rattled by time pressure, display great patience and turn time into an ally.

6. Ask lots of questions. Above average negotiators ask twice as many questions as average negotiators. Questions uncover needs, provide information, diffuse conflict, persuade and keep you in control.

7. Actively listen. Professional negotiators listen intently and don't get distracted by emotions. They build rapport and demonstrate understanding by reflecting the content and feelings of the other party. To keep the negotiation on track they regularly summarise where they are at.

8. Assert your needs. Effective negotiators use assertive rather than aggressive or passive language to state clearly what they want, feel and think. Assertive speakers assert their needs by choosing words and body language which convey strength and authority.

9. Probe with conditional proposals. Skilled negotiators probe for areas of movement with brief, tentative proposals. They make fewer instant counter-proposals, rarely say no and regularly summarise areas of agreement.

10. Explore lots of options. Effective negotiators try to increase the number of variables, as each new variable creates more options for mutual gain. The more variables, the better the chance of a win-win settlement.

11. Start high, concede slowly. Winning negotiators consistently aim higher, create room to move and concede slowly with small concessions at a controlled rate. And they always make sure the other side reciprocates.

12. Verify what has been agreed to. Top negotiators never leave the negotiating table without going back over every point of the agreement. They summarise every point on paper and make plans for meetings to settle future differences.

13. Review your performance. Skilled negotiators learn from their mistakes. They go back over the negotiation looking for areas to improve.

14. Build long-term working relationships. Successful negotiators practice the three R's of relationship building. They continue to be *reliable, rational* and *receptive* – regardless of how the other side behaves.

15. Maximize your power. Like a skilled card player negotiators know how to play a poor hand. For them power is largely a state of mind – a matter of perception.

16. Adapt your strategy to fit the situation. The best negotiators are win-win motivated. They are constructive, explore options for mutual gain and try to satisfy both sides' interests. However, they are first and foremost adaptable, they adjust their strategy and tactics to fit the situation.

Recommendations for Further Reading

If you still have an appetite to read more on negotiation, I recommend the following titles.

Cohen, Herb: *You Can Negotiate Anything*. Angus and Robertson, London, 1982; Lyle Stuart, Secaucus, New Jersey, 1980.

The most readable, racy guide on negotiation there is, with lots of amusing anecdotes. Cohen knows how to negotiate, is street smart, and shows it. Unfortunately the book concentrates on strategies, tactics and ploys to the virtual exclusion of everything else.

Fisher, Roger & Ury, William: *Getting to Yes*. Century Hutchinson, London, 1983; Houghton Mifflin, Boston, 1981.

The best introduction to joint problem solving available. Some of Fisher's and Ury's guiding principles – focus on interests not positions, develop a BATNA, invent options for mutual gain – should be drilled into every trainee negotiator. An essential read and highly readable too.

Fisher, Roger & Brown, Scott: *Getting Together*. Century Hutchinson, London; Houghton Mifflin, Boston, 1988.

The sequel to *Getting to Yes, Getting Together* shows how to build long-term relationships that really work. Full of common sense which, unfortunately, is not so common.

Jandt, Fred E.: *Win-Win Negotiating*. Wiley, New York, 1985.

Fred Jandt has conducted seminars on conflict management and negotiation for thousands of executives. His principles for handling conflict are practical, constructive and applicable to all types of conflict.

Karrass, Chester L.: *Give & Take*. Thomas Y. Crowell, New York, 1974.

If you're buying or selling and want to brush up on your knowledge of the dozens of tactics used, then this is the book. Unfortunately, the A to Z organisation of the material makes it more difficult rather than easier to use.

Kennedy, Gavin: *Everything is Negotiable*. Arrow Books, London, 1984; Prentice Hall, Englewood Cliffs, New Jersey.

A highly readable examination of the common problems negotiators face and how to handle them. The book is illustrated with scores of examples drawn from the world of international business. Anything Gavin Kennedy writes on negotiation is worth reading.

Kennedy, Gavin, Benson, John & McMillan, John: *Managing Negotiations*. Century Hutchinson, London; Prentice Hall, Englewood Cliffs, New Jersey, 1980.

Gavin Kennedy, John Benson and John McMillan break the negotiation process into eight steps and explore the different skills and techniques used in each. Contains lots of useful tips.

Kennedy, Gavin: *Pocket Negotiator*. Basil Blackwell, Oxford and The Economist Publications, London; Basil Blackwell, New York, 1987.

Organised like a dictionary, every serious negotiator should own a copy of this invaluable desk guide.

Lax, David A. & Sebenius, James K.: *The Manager as Negotiator: Bargaining for co-operation and competitive gain*. Free Press Inc., New York; Collier Macmillan, London, 1987.

This is the definitive guide on how managers negotiate. Used as a text in many business school courses, this book is one of the few that deserves to be read two or three times.

Checklist of Body Language Gestures

One of the biggest mistakes you can make in observing body language is to make judgements on the basis of a solitary gesture. Gestures come in clusters and should always be interpreted this way.

Openness

- warm smile
- unfolded arms
- uncrossed legs
- leaning forward
- relaxed body
- direct eye contact with dilated pupils
- open palms
- unbuttoned/removed coat (for men)
- hand/s to chest (for men)

Defensiveness

- little eye contact
- corners of lips turned down

- rigid body
- clenched hands
- palm-to-back-of-neck
- tightly crossed arms
- wrinkled brow
- tight pursed lips
- head down
- tightly crossed legs/ankles
- scratching below earlobes or side of neck

Dominance

- palms down
- straddling a chair – sitting with the chair back serving as a shield
- feet on desk
- physical elevation above the other person
- strident, loud voice
- leaning back in chair with both hands supporting head
- strong palm-down thrusting or knuckle crunching handshake
- leg over arm of chair
- using desk as a physical barrier

Agressiveness

- furrowed brow
- sustained eye contact with contracted pupils (stare)

- pointing glasses
- clenched fist/s
- arms spread out while hands grip the edge of table
- leg over arm of chair
- squinting of the eyes
- downward turned eyebrows
- pointed index finger
- strong palm-down thrusting or knuckle crunching handshake
- hands-on-hips when standing
- moving in on the other person's personal territory

Boredom or Indifference

- blank stare
- lack of eye blinking
- head in palm of hand
- repetitive finger or foot tapping
- little eye contact
- drooping eyes
- crossed legs
- doodling

Frustration

- staring into space
- running fingers through hair

- kicking at ground or imaginary object
- short in-and-out breaths
- wringing of hands
- tightly closed lips
- rubbing back of neck
- taking deep breaths
- tightly clenched hands
- pacing

Readiness

- good eye contact
- seated, leaning forward with hands on the mid thigh or knees
- lively facial expression
- standing with coat open and pushed back with hands on hips (for men)
- alert facial expression
- close proximity
- sitting on edge of chair
- nodding in agreement

Confidence

- steepling of hands (joining fingers like a church steeple)
- feet on desk
- leaning back with hands joined behind back of head
- proud erect stance with hands joined behind back

- head up
- stretched legs
- physically elevating oneself
- leaning back in chair
- continuous eye contact
- chin forward

Nervousness, Uncertainty

- weak, clammy handshake
- constant throat clearing
- hands covering mouth while speaking
- poor eye contact
- nervous laughter
- tapping fingers on table
- sighing
- crossed arms and legs
- fidgeting in chair
- fiddling with objects, clothing
- pacing
- smoking
- biting or picking finger nails or cuticles

Checkpoints:
Steps One to Seven

Step One:
Ready Yourself

Checkpoints:

- Develop a BATNA.

- Identify your interests.

- Identify your opponent's interests.

- List, rank and value the issues.

- Gather information.

- Analyse the other party.

- Role play.

- Test your assumptions.

- Plan your agenda.

- Consult with others.

- Determine the limits of your authority.

- Determine your first offer.

- Choose your team members.

- Devise a time plan.

- Choose a venue.

- Plan your strategy.

- Choose appropriate tactics.

Step Two:
Exploring Each Other's Needs

Checkpoints:

- Communicate your opening position.

- Discover your opponent's position.

- Ask lots of questions.

- Start with open questions.

- Finish with closed questions.

- Avoid destructive questions.

- Reflect the content of the other side.

- Reflect the other side's feelings.

- Summarise where you are at.

- Create a positive, open non-verbal climate.

- Speak clearly and confidently.

- Use assertive language.

- Use silence for effect.

- Translate the meta-talk.

Step Three:
Signalling for Movement

Checkpoints:

■ Listen intently for signals showing movement.

■ Clarify all signals with follow up questions.

■ Reciprocate with your own signals.

■ Repeat or reword missed signals.

Step Four:
Probing with Proposals

Checkpoints:

- Probe to elicit information.

- Use proposals to clarify priorities.

- Propose, then go quiet.

- State your condition first and be specific.

- Use the if/then technique.

- Never interrupt a proposal.

- Don't instantly reject a proposal.

- Avoid the proposal killer "I disagree".

- Don't immediately counter with your own proposal.

- Give as detailed a response as possible.

- Indicate areas of agreement.

- Regularly summarise where you are at.

- Repackage proposals to make them more acceptable.

- Multiply the variables to create more options and win-win packages.

Step Five:
Exchanging Concessions

Checkpoints:

- Link issues, don't trade piecemeal.
- Give yourself plenty of room to negotiate.
- If you're selling, start high.
- If you're buying, start low.
- All offers should be realistic and credible.
- Avoid making the first major concession.
- Trade reluctantly.
- Make small concessions.
- Make sure the other side reciprocates.
- Control and monitor your concession rate.
- Concede slowly.
- Conserve concessions for last minute trades.
- Preface all offers with a condition.
- Justify all concessions.
- Track all concessions – yours and theirs.
- Build momentum by emphasising common interests.
- Reward, don't punish, concessions.
- Don't turn minor issues into matters of principle.
- Shift issues at impasses.
- Handle ridiculous offers with care.

Step Six:
Closing the Deal

Checkpoints:

- Decide at what point you want to stop trading.

- Assess whether it is the right time.

- Look out for body language cues.

- Listen for questions which indicate a readiness to close.

- Test the waters with a trial close.

- Start with a summary close.

- If necessary consider other possible closes.

- Guard against deadline pressures.

- Use body language to project a confident image.

- Try to anticipate and avoid last minute deadlocks.

- Consider changing the negotiator or using a mediator.

- Keep questioning and listening.

Step Seven:
Tying Up the Loose Ends

Checkpoints:

- Verify what has been agreed to.

- Put the agreement in writing.

- Volunteer to do the writing.

- Write the agreement in plain explicit language.

- Question every ambiguity.

- Write up the agreement before separating.

- Plan for future differences.

- Review your performance.

References

1. Rubin, J. Z. *Negotiation*. 27 American Behavioural Scientists, Sage Publications, pp. 135, 135–137, 140–142 (1983).
2. Produced by permission Doug Malouf, Australian Real Estate Consultant.
3. Cheryl Moch & Vincent Virga, *Deals*, Crown Publishers, New York, 1984, pp. 40–43.
4. Wriggens, W., "Up for Auction: Malta Bargains with Great Britain, 1971." In William Zartman (ed.), *The 50% Solution*, Anchor Doubleday, Garden City, N.Y., 1976.
5. Christine Harvey, *Secrets of the World's Top Sales Performers*, Business Books Limited, London, 1989, p. 50.
6. Akio Morita with Edwin M. Reingold and Mitsuko Shimomura, *Made in Japan. Akio Morita and Sony,* Collins, London, 1987, pp. 84–86.
7. Leonard M. Fuld, *Monitoring the Competition, Find Out What's Really Going On Over There,* John Wiley, New York, pp. 49–50.
8. J. Carter, *Keeping Faith: Memoirs of a President,* Collins, London, 1982, p. 320.
9. Earl Brooks & George S. Odiorne, *Managing by Negotiation*, Van Nostrand Reinhold, New York, 1984, p. 77.
10. Donald J. Trump with Tony Schwartz, *Trump, The Art of the Deal,* Warner Books, New York, 1987, pp. 140–141.
11. William L. Ury, *Beyond the Hotline,* Penguin Books, New York, 1986, p. 37.
12. Quoted in Charles Ikle, *How Nations Negotiate,* Harper & Row, New York, 1964.
13. Neil Rackham, *Account Strategy for Major Sales,* Gower, Aldershot, Hampshire, 1988, p. 143.

14. Neil Rackham, *Making Major Sales*, Gower, Aldershot, Hampshire, 1987, p. 27.

15. Jacques Lalanne, *Attack by Question*, Psychology Today Magazine, Ziff Davis, 1975.

16. Peter Farb, *Word Play*, Bantam Books, New York, 1973, pp. 240–241.

17. Albert Mehrabian, *Silent Messages*, Wadsworth Publishing, Belmont, California, 1982.

18. Janet Elsea, *First Impression Best Impression*, Fireside Edition, Simon & Schuster, New York, 1985, p. 11.

19. Albert Mehrabian, *Non Verbal Communication*, Aldine-Atherton, Chicago, 1972.

20. G. Egan, *From You and Me: The Skills of Communicating and Relating to Others*, Wadsworth Publishing, Belmont, California, 1977.

21. Gerard I. Nierenberg and Henry H. Calero, *How to Read a Person Like a Book*, Thorsons, Wellingborough, Northamptonshire, 1973, p. 19.

22. Gerard I. Nierenberg and Henry H. Calero, *How to Read a Person Like a Book*, Thorsons, Wellingborough, Northamptonshire, 1973, p. 39.

23. Suzette Haden Elgin, *Success with the Gentle Art of Verbal Self Defense*, Prentice Hall, Englewood Cliffs, New Jersey, 1989, p. 4.

24. Janet Elsea, *First Impression, Best Impression*, Simon & Schuster, New York, 1985.

25. Findings summarised in Gavin Kennedy, *The Economist Pocket Negotiator*, Basil Blackwell, Economist Publications, Oxford and London, 1987, p. 153.

26. Chester L. Karrass, *The Negotiating Game*, Thomas Y. Crowell, New York, 1970, pp. 18–20.

27. Chester L. Karrass, *Give and Take*, Thomas Y. Crowell, New York, 1974, p. 177.

28. *Fortune International*, Time Inc, New York, November 6, 1989, p. 92.

29. Roger Fisher and Scott Brown, *Getting Together*, Houghton Mifflin, New York, 1988, p. XI.

30. Lawrence Susskind and Jeffrey Cruikshank, *Breaking the Impasse*, Basic Books, New York, 1987, pp. 91–92.

31. *Peter Freuchen's Book of the Eskimos*, Ed. Dagmar Freuchen, The World Publishing Company, Cleveland, Ohio, 1961, pp. 72–78.

32. *Fortune International,* Time Inc, New York, Dec. 4, 1989, p. 69.

33. Robert B. Cialdini, *Influence: The New Psychology of Modern Persuasion,* William Morrow, New York, 1984, p. 208.

34. David A. Lax, James K. Sebenius, *The Manager as Negotiator,* The Free Press, New York, 1986, pp. 117–118.

35. *Fortune International*, Time Inc, New York, Sept. 25, 1989, p. 86.

36. Cited in Robert B. Cialdini, *Influence*, William Morrow, New York, 1984, p. 166.

37. Example provided by Roger Fisher & William Ury, *Getting to Yes*, Century Hutchinson, London, pp. 42–43.

38. Gavin Kennedy, *Pocket Negotiator*, Basil Blackwell and The Economist Publications, Oxford and London, 1987, p. 118.

39. Gavin Kennedy, *Everything is Negotiable*, Arrow Books, London, 1984, p. 302.

Index

Training Seminars

Sometimes it's easier and quicker to develop negotiation skills by attending a training programme.

If you are interested in further information on training programmes based on this book contact:

The Mills Group
P O Box 30-818
Lower Hutt
New Zealand

Tel 64-4-569-6744
Fax 64-4-569-7464
Email Harry@millsgp.co.nz